Cambridge Elements ≡

Elements in Global China
edited by
Ching Kwan Lee
University of California–Los Angeles

CHINA IN GLOBAL HEALTH

Past and Present

Mary Augusta Brazelton
University of Cambridge

CAMBRIDGE
UNIVERSITY PRESS

Shaftesbury Road, Cambridge CB2 8EA, United Kingdom

One Liberty Plaza, 20th Floor, New York, NY 10006, USA

477 Williamstown Road, Port Melbourne, VIC 3207, Australia

314–321, 3rd Floor, Plot 3, Splendor Forum, Jasola District Centre,
New Delhi – 110025, India

103 Penang Road, #05–06/07, Visioncrest Commercial, Singapore 238467

Cambridge University Press is part of Cambridge University Press & Assessment,
a department of the University of Cambridge.

We share the University's mission to contribute to society through the pursuit of
education, learning and research at the highest international levels of excellence.

www.cambridge.org
Information on this title: www.cambridge.org/9781009045667

DOI: 10.1017/9781009042666

First published 2023

A catalogue record for this publication is available from the British Library.

ISBN 978-1-009-04566-7 Paperback
ISSN 2632-7341 (online)
ISSN 2632-7333 (print)

China in Global Health

Past and Present

Elements in Global China

DOI: 10.1017/9781009042666
First published online: January 2023

Mary Augusta Brazelton
University of Cambridge

Author for correspondence: Mary Augusta Brazelton, mab94@cam.ac.uk

Abstract: This Element argues that the territories and peoples associated with China have played vital roles in the emergence of modern international health. In the early twentieth century, repeated epidemic outbreaks in China justified interventions by transnational organisations; these projects shaped strategies for international health. China has also served as a space of creativity and reinvention, in which administrators developed new models of health care during decades of war and revolution, even as traditional practitioners presented alternatives to Western biomedicine. The 1949 establishment of the People's Republic of China introduced a new era of socialist internationalism, as well as new initiatives to establish connections across the non-aligned world using medical diplomacy. After 1978, the post-socialist transition gave rise to new configurations of health governance. The rich and varied history of Chinese involvement in global health offers a means to make sense of present-day crises.

Keywords: China, global health, international health, history of medicine, public health

ISBNs: 9781009045667 (PB), 9781009042666 (OC)
ISSNs: 2632-7341 (online), 2632-7333 (print)

Contents

1 Introduction: China and the Making of Global Health

In the twenty-first century, public health is increasingly studied and understood in international terms. What we now call 'global health' is a product of recent historical processes generating an area of research and practice that treats the health of populations in a planetary context. This Element argues that there is no global health without China. The territories and peoples associated with China have played vital roles in the emergence of this discipline, and they remain central to its policies and practices. This significance is a consequence of two connected but contrasting functions: widespread understandings of China as a place where infectious diseases originate; but also the active agency of Chinese peoples in identifying new ways to control and end epidemics.

It is therefore possible to tell two stories about China's role in events shaping modern international health, one dark, one light. In the former, repeated epidemic outbreaks in the early twentieth century justified interventions by transnational organisations; these projects on Chinese soil shaped subsequent mid-century strategies to manage the health of the world's populations, but largely came to an end after the Chinese Communist Party (CCP) took control of mainland China. After 1978, a post-socialist transition gave rise to new configurations of health governance that eventually created the conditions for Covid-19 to become a global pandemic in 2020. In this narrative, which has generally predominated in anglophone scholarship, China and Chinese actors have remained marginal to the history of international and global health. Recent textbooks and overviews have generally focused on familiar institutions and Euro–American actors in China: the League of Nations, the Rockefeller Foundation, the Pan-American Health Organisation, and the World Health Organization (WHO) (Palmer 2010; Packard 2016; Cueto, Brown, and Fee 2019; Cueto 2020).

Yet that story leaves significant gaps. Early twentieth-century epidemics also contributed to the establishment of a domestic community of globally engaged biomedical researchers. Considering Chinese perspectives in conjunction with familiar tales suggests that China has indeed served as a space of epidemic genesis, but also of creativity and reinvention, in which administrators developed new models of health care during mid-twentieth-century decades of war and revolution even as traditional practitioners presented alternatives to Western biomedicine. The 1949 establishment of the People's Republic of China (PRC) introduced a new era of socialist internationalism, marked by participation in Soviet-led health programmes as well as Chinese initiatives to establish connections across the non-aligned world using medical diplomacy. The rich and varied history of Chinese involvement in global health – replete with stories both light and dark – thus offers a means to make sense of present-day crises.

What was China? This is a complex question, since across the twentieth century, the peoples, languages, and territories identified as Chinese underwent manifold radical transformations. The schism between the PRC and the Republic of China on Taiwan (ROC); the emancipation of Hong Kong from British rule; and the wavering and uncertain status of 'Overseas Chinese' as a category incorporating not only those who returned to the PRC during the Cold War from communities in Indonesia and elsewhere but also those who left for North America, Europe, and other distant shores (Kuhn 2008; Zhou 2019): the diversity of these experiences suggests that there is not one China, or Chinese people. Likewise, the sovereign borders allegedly demarcating 'China' reveal remarkable ethnic, linguistic, and cultural range, from aboriginal Taiwanese communities to the many minority peoples of Yunnan, Xinjiang, and other border provinces. And in the conversations connecting China, Chinese culture, and Chinese medicine, all too often a uniform view of 'China' is assumed (Zhan 2009, 191). Here, I attempt to discuss the variety of communities identifying as Sinophone (Chinese-speaking) – but because much of the available literature focuses on the PRC, that polity unavoidably dominates the discussions that follow.

Several key themes provide connecting strands. One is the secular trend over the twentieth century that is sometimes described as China's demographic transition: a propitious decrease in death rates and increasing longevity. The reliability of statistics from the PRC is a complicated question (Banister 1987; Ghosh 2020), but the trend seems clear. In the history of medicine, this is sometimes depicted in epidemiological terms: a fall in infectious disease incidence, coupled with a rise in chronic disease morbidity and mortality. These trends have consequences for how we understand China's role in international and global health. First, they indicate the changing role played by China in the global origin and spread of epidemics: a sharp decline in transmission over the twentieth century has been countered by the emergence in recent decades of novel influenzas and coronaviruses. Second, they indicate the transformation of the PRC from a state that received foreign aid to one that distributed it, as domestic health systems gained global recognition for their successes. Third, they indicate shifting priorities for Chinese health systems – of significant consequence for global medical research.

Another integrative theme involves the rich medical pluralism that has characterised decision-making around health in Sinophone populations. Foreign observers have been quick to attribute the distinctive features of Chinese responses to Covid-19 to 'Confucian culture' or the authoritarian nature of the PRC state – but such glib generalisations gloss over a variety of attitudes and beliefs that shaped epidemic responses and health administration throughout the twentieth century. Simple dichotomies between Chinese and Western medicine would be misleading here, since ideas about medicine and modernity became fundamentally intertwined in the Chinese context during the early twentieth century and Chinese medical professions coalesced through conflict with physicians trained in Euro–American traditions (Lei 2014). In the early twentieth century, international health became an arena for contestation between medical practitioners trained in different traditions over the authority to represent China on a global stage. In the Cold War, initiatives to 'combine Chinese and Western medicine' implicitly codified the dichotomies they allegedly sought to overturn. And in the post-socialist period, the transgression of animal–human boundaries in wildlife farming, partly in the service of an expanding Chinese pharmaceutical industry, gave rise to global concerns about zoonotic disease transmission conceptualised in biomedical frameworks.

A third connecting strand, then, is that of the importance of interspecies relationships to both the emergence and management of infectious diseases. Observers of Covid-19 and other recent epidemics in China have pointed to the significance of dynamics linking humans, animals, and pathogens, in which transgressive encounters between wild animals and middle-class consumers have eluded the reach of health administration with pathogenic results (Zhan 2005; Evans 2020; Keck 2020). Yet the history of public health in China reveals alternative understandings of the relationships connecting humans, animals, and environments. It reminds us that the pernicious dynamics that led to intensive industrial farming and the cultivation of wildlife, which created the conditions in which novel pathogens could arise, are the result of global social and economic processes. It also suggests that interspecies entanglements in China have positively contributed to public health structures and strategies.

This Element builds on existing scholarship on the history of global health and the history of medicine in China. Like definitions of China and Chineseness, the meanings and scope of public, international, and global health have changed over time. In what follows, I seek to use terms appropriate for the period under consideration. 'Public health' was formulated in the nineteenth century as a set of relations between medicine and society concerned with sanitary reforms and infectious disease control; in the late twentieth century, historians interpreted the concept in expansive ways, incorporating more perspectives and temporalities. The scholar Dorothy Porter offers a useful definition of public health as 'the history of collective action in relation to the health of populations' (Porter 1999, 4). In the late nineteenth and early twentieth centuries, the term 'international health' was commonly understood to encompass discussions and activities relating to the coordination of epidemic response and control across national and imperial borders. It was only in the 1990s that the term 'global health' began to replace 'international health', referring to efforts to prioritise the health of the entire planet's population over national interests (Brown, Cueto, and Fee 2006, 62).

The history of international health thus finds its origins in colonial medicine and imperial neglect (Bashford 2004; Harrison 2016; Pearson 2018). Yet its projects also fostered revolutionary nationalism and anti-colonial socialist internationalism (Waitzkin et al. 2001; Lo 2002; Anderson and Pols 2012; Solomon 2017; Pols 2018). Recent histories of global health have understandably tended to focus on key organisations in the Global North that have declared their mission to improve the health of the world's populations, most notably the Rockefeller Foundation and the World Health Organization; in this respect they have still put Westerners at the centre of the story (Palmer 2010; Packard 2016; Cueto, Brown, and Fee 2019). The result has been an incomplete picture of the role of China in international and global health. While familiar characters and organisations from canonical narratives do appear in the following pages, sometimes prominently, this Element seeks to give primacy to Chinese perspectives.

To understand those perspectives, and the history of China's role in international and global health more generally, it is necessary to survey the ways in which health and medicine became central to governance there. Here, a fourth overarching theme of the Element emerges, which follows the intensification of biopolitical relationships between Chinese states and peoples over the twentieth century. By 'biopolitics', I refer to the Foucauldian concept that perceives populations and their biologies as a central concern of governments (Campbell and Sitze 2013, 14). This Element is concerned with the specific roles that biopolitical approaches to governance have played in Chinese contexts, especially the growing strength of biopower over the twentieth century. In this respect, it builds on important previous scholarship. Ruth Rogaski has traced how, from the mid-nineteenth-century establishment of hyper-colonial treaty ports, the concept of *weisheng* connected a variety of hygienic practices to Prussian and Japanese concepts of public health. In these dynamics, the state exerted *biopower*: control over and regulation of its population's health (Rogaski 2004). David Luesink has argued that Chinese concepts of political anatomy in which the body provided a mirror for the state supported advocacy for the adoption of anatomical knowledge by early twentieth-century medical professionals. This development in turn laid the foundations for an 'anatomo-politics' in which the state established power over individual bodies (Luesink 2017). In the early twentieth century, across Asia, scientists and physicians constituted an important group among nationalist revolutionaries. Hans Pols and Warwick Anderson suggest that scientific training facilitated a kind of anticolonial sentiment that was distinct from literary or historicist forms of nationalism (Anderson and Pols 2012, 97).

The history of medicine in twentieth-century China reveals not only the ways in which governance became intertwined with health, but also the increasing prominence that medicine occupied in international relations. At the beginning of the century, a 1905 article labelling China the 'Sick Man of the Far East' appeared in the *New York Times*. This parallel with nineteenth-century descriptions of the Ottoman Empire as the 'Sick Man of Europe' described the political vulnerability of the Qing dynasty, China's last imperial regime, to predation by European powers (The Sick Man of the Far East 1905; Amelung 2020, 9). Over the course of the century, medicine moved from the realm of metaphor to become a more direct concern of foreign policy. As we will see in Section 1.2, the 1910 outbreak of pneumonic plague in north-east China sparked Russian and Japanese imperial adventures into Qing territory, and in the Second World War epidemics spurred a variety of foreign aid donations and interventions. Erez Manela has argued that the case of smallpox eradication demonstrates the importance of public health to diplomatic history in the Cold War context (Manela 2010, 301–2). And upon the 2020 outbreak of Covid-19, the re-emergence of accusations calling China the 'sick man of Asia' sparked a vigorous backlash from representatives of the PRC (Rogaski 2021).

The following discussion proceeds broadly chronologically through the twentieth century. A longer view might have delved further into early and early modern epidemic management, or the history of missionary medicine in China, or regional networks of medical exchange in East and South-East Asia. Likewise, constraints of space preclude giving due attention to the significance of histories of mental health, sexuality, or disability in the narratives surveyed. This Element instead focuses on epidemic and infectious diseases in the more recent past as a period of remarkable social and medical transformation across the Sinophone world. Sections 1.1, 1.2, and 1.3 consider the end of the Qing dynasty and the early years of the Republic that succeeded it, an era largely marked by political infighting and regional warlord separatism. The second section considers the ambitious projects of the 'Nanjing Decade', the period between 1927 and 1937 when the Nationalist Party consolidated control over the Republican state in central and coastal regions. The third section discusses international commitments in public health by the PRC and ROC governments in the Cold War era, and the fourth section places current trends in the management of Covid-19 in the context of the recent history of post-socialism in the PRC and exclusion from global health governance in Taiwan.

1.1 Defining Medicine in China

The establishment of the modern Chinese nation state in the early twentieth century was inextricably tied up with early collaborations in international health. The crumbling Qing empire used public health to grasp at power when a deadly epidemic broke out in the north-eastern ancestral homeland of its rulers. And men trained in Western medicine – a profession that some chose for its symbolic significance, with attendant imagery of healing the nation as a body – played key roles in the Xinhai Revolution which ended that empire. The novel practices and theories of hygiene they studied sought to address the epidemics then prevalent in East Asia; in so doing, they came into conflict with the great range of medical traditions that had long been in use in China.

A diversity of medical traditions existed among Chinese-speaking peoples by the year 1900. Learned physicians drew on knowledge of medical classics such as *The Yellow Emperor's Inner Canon* (*Huangdi neijing* 皇帝內經) or the *Golden Mirror of Medicine* (*Yuzuan yizong jinjian* 御纂醫宗金鑑) (see Figure 1). They trained through extensive apprenticeships, often reflecting prestigious medical lineages. A lack of regulation meant that physicians using herbal medicine, acupuncture, and/or moxibustion competed with specialists in surgery, women's disorders, and other sub-fields in a thriving and decentralised medical marketplace. Travelling folk healers offered fortune-telling services, sold drugs, and offered prayers, and massage therapists and tooth-pullers also offered their wares in this realm (Andrews 2013, 211).

At the turn of the century, these traditions had already encountered what became known as Western medicine, mainly through the intervention of Christian missionaries. Like 'Chinese medicine', the term 'Western medicine' lent seeming coherence to a diversity of approaches to medical theories and practices. Members of the Jesuit order had arrived in China in the 1580s, and once ensconced at the Qing court they imported drugs, treated patients, instructed emperors in anatomical knowledge, and translated medical texts into Chinese and Manchu (Asen 2009; Golvers 2011; Puente-Ballesteros 2011). In the nineteenth century, Protestant missionary organisations came to the forefront of medical interventions, establishing hospitals and medical schools in treaty ports forced open to foreign trade by the Opium Wars (Choa 1990; Minden 1994; Andrews 2014, 51–68). Especially after the 1838 formation of the Medical Missionary Society in China, but also through the European and American missionary societies that had recruited them, physicians stationed at missions across China tapped into a network of transnational colonial medicine, complete with its own publications, funding structures, and recruitment procedures (Choa 1990, 16–18; Lazich 2006). The research supported by this

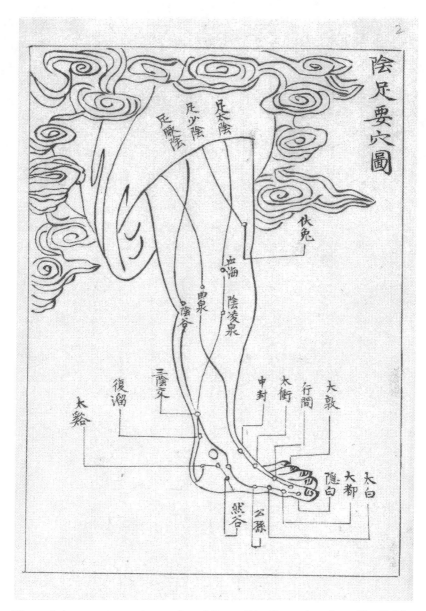

Figure 1 Acupuncture points and meridians of the foot, taken from *The Golden Mirror of Medicine*, first published in 1742. Image courtesy Wellcome Collection, attribution 4.0 International (CC BY 4.0).

network proved formative to the establishment of tropical medicine, a novel discipline that relied on access to experimental subjects in colonies in the service of the expansion of imperial power. It was during his time as a surgeon for the Chinese Maritime Customs Service, for example, that the British physician Patrick Manson developed theories of parasitic disease transmission, eventually earning the moniker 'father of tropical medicine'; the Customs Service was an administrative product of the Opium Wars, staffed by foreign agents who supervised the collection of taxes at treaty ports (Haynes 2001). In southern China, French physicians established consular hospitals and Pasteur Institutes as part of a strategy to establish imperial influence across the region bordering French Indochina (Bretelle-Establet 1999; Liu 2017; Velmet 2020).

These French doctors made use of long-established pathways. Europe was, of course, not the only region to have a history of medical exchanges with China. Although it is generally assumed that Chinese medical traditions exerted a dominant influence over surrounding regions, South-East Asia was a significant source as well as a destination of knowledge and drugs for Chinese physicians (Thompson 2015). Likewise, Inner Asia was an enduring site for exchanges of medical knowledge between the continent's eastern and western peripheries (Nappi 2009; van Vleet 2015). To the east, as early as the eleventh century, the Korean state of Koryŏ had received medical literature and physician-emissaries from China's Southern Song Dynasty; in return, it provided the Song with rare Chinese medical texts which had been lost there (Chai and Ch'ae 2017, 36–8). Likewise, Japanese physicians had avidly consumed and translated classical Chinese medical texts since at least the early modern period (Elman 2008); by the early twentieth century, as we shall see, Japan had become a crucial site for Chinese students' and writers' exposure to novel medical practices and theories. A broad definition of 'international health' might extend to consider these regional circuits of influence and exchange, as well as more traditional disciplinary networks and organisations.

In contrast to the long-established networks of exchange described above, in European-led transnational sanitary discourses of the early twentieth century, China figured primarily as a dangerous zone harbouring deadly infections. The Qing was maligned for its inattention to sanitation and public health. For example, the proceedings of the 1881 International Sanitary Conference in Washington, DC criticised health in China, saying, 'The only sanitary measures taken in this country are quarantine measures against the importation of cholera' (International Sanitary Conference 1881, 176). And in a discussion of plague in China and India that took place in 1897 during an International Sanitary Conference in Venice, the proceedings noted that 'The English authorities [of Hong Kong] have made laudable efforts to lessen the ravages of the scourge. But the Chinese offer great resistance to the application of hygiene and disinfection measures' (International Sanitary Conference 1897, 317).

It would be inaccurate, however, to say that there were no state-sponsored health initiatives whatsoever in China. For instance, the Song dynasty

(960–1279 CE) saw the establishment and strengthening of state medical institutions and publications, as well as epidemic relief (Hinrichs 2013, 99–102). Much later, the Qing state, under a reform-minded administration, established a Sanitary Office in 1905 as part of a new Ministry of Police. This office took responsibility for inspecting pharmacies, licensing physicians, and a range of other hygienic tasks from street sweeping to epidemic prevention. In the following year, an Office of Health Care assumed new responsibilities for inspecting food and drink, as well as administering public health among the poor, in factories, and in theatres. A Quarantine Department oversaw the prevention of infectious diseases via immunisation against smallpox and enforcing isolation policies, and a Medical Department oversaw the registration of physicians. In 1906, a public hospital opened in the capital of Beijing, with success (Zhu and Cao 2009, 128–33).

These efforts were significant in part because the Opium Wars had subjected the Qing to predation by numerous Euro–American powers. As Ruth Rogaski has shown, the resulting hyper-colonial dynamic led to the establishment of 'hygienic modernity' in China's treaty ports: a set of practices which sought to impose public health in a way that reinforced colonial frameworks and their connections to state biopower, as well as discourses of Chinese deficiency within these frameworks (Rogaski 2004). Growing frustration with the impoverished and weak state of the Qing by the late nineteenth century led many intellectuals to see their empire's relationship to other countries in terms of national competition, just at a time when the translation of texts on evolution and especially social Darwinism articulated the significance of the 'survival of the fittest'. They perceived a need for legal and social revolution to enable China to compete among the fittest in a global social order (So 2012; Carrai 2019, 95). So, the reception of eugenics in China made public health relevant to international relations, by virtue of the idea that a healthy population was necessary for China to compete successfully with the empires that had recently extracted so much from the Qing. For instance, Kang Youwei (康有為) and Liang Qichao (梁啓超) promoted early marriage, prenatal care, women's education, and sterilisation of those who should not reproduce as part of the Self-Strengthening Movement, an attempt to make strategic use of Western learning in order to strengthen the military and the economy against foreign encroachment (Chung 2014, 795–7).

Although reform-minded intellectuals in China thus engaged with the long-term challenges facing the Qing, short-term questions of transnational public health remained pressing at the turn of the twentieth century. International health at this time targeted the failures of national governments to prevent epidemics, especially cholera, from spreading across national and imperial borders. A series of International Sanitary Conferences had been convened for this purpose since the 1850s, and many of their discussions blamed non-Western states for failing to keep diseases within their territories. The Qing occasionally sent representatives to these conferences, even though European delegates dominated the conversation. For example, in 1881 Chen Lanbin (陳蘭彬), the first Qing ambassador to the United States, attended an International Sanitary Conference in Washington, DC (Chen 2018, 345). Several years later, the diplomat and Self-Strengthener Chen Jitong (陈季同) participated in the International Sanitary Conference held at Rome in 1885 (International Sanitary Conference 1885, 64–5).

The many epidemic diseases that afflicted China in the early twentieth century made it an important site for both medical crisis and discovery. In 1894, Alexandre Yersin and Kitasato Shibasaburō (北里 柴三郎) competed to discover the causative agent of the bubonic plague outbreak devastating the British colony of Hong Kong. Shibasaburō, the Japanese student of Robert Koch, was first to identify and publish on the plague bacillus, but Yersin, the Swiss student of Louis Pasteur, provided a more accurate description and pure cultures of what came to be known as *Yersinia pestis*, as well as a conjecture that rats were involved in the transmission of plague (Echenberg 2007, 34–5). The plague exposed and amplified tensions between the city's Chinese and European populations. Official efforts to disinfect buildings in Chinese communities and remove infected patients to isolation hospitals provoked fear, flight, and resistance. Despite the mediating intervention of the Tung Wah Hospital Committee, a charitable organisation run by Chinese merchants, these conflicts persisted until the easing of the epidemic in the autumn of 1894. Throughout the crisis, colonial officials were concerned with stopping the flow of disease – but *not* money, goods, or labour – through the city (Peckham 2016, 83–9).

While British officials fretted over plague in Hong Kong, Chinese colonial subjects posed new medical challenges for an entirely different imperial government. Following the 1895 defeat of China in the First Sino–Japanese War, the island of Taiwan, formerly a province of the Qing Dynasty, was relegated to Japanese rule. Its new overlords promptly applied the model that Japan's home islands had adopted in the 1870s, based on mid-nineteenth-century German centralised systems that emphasised sanitary police and public hygiene via quarantine stations and public hospitals. The perceived success of this process made Taiwan a model for Japanese colonial medicine in Korea, Sakhalin, and other holdings (Liu 2009, 54–60). Over time, as the empire expanded, Japanese administrators sought to institute 'scientific colonialism' in Taiwan as part of a distinctively Asian civilising mission. Colonial medicine constituted a major plan within this strategy to bring science to the island, yet its successful establishment led to the formation of an elite profession of Taiwanese physicians who pursued anti-colonial politics after the establishment of civil rule in 1919 (Lo 2002, 5).

This section has surveyed medicine and public health in Sinophone regions at the beginning of the twentieth century. It has called attention to the diverse range of medical traditions in play, the complex configurations of imperial power and subjugation of Chinese-identifying people, and the ways in which medicine was already caught up in long-established transnational networks even before new epidemiological crises brought China into the ambit of European anxieties over cross-border disease transmission. At the close of the century's first decade, a novel epidemic would bring the Qing dynasty to a newly prominent position of concern and research in international health.

1.2 Fighting Plague and Asserting Authority in Manchuria

In 1910, plague emerged in the region of north-east Asia then called Manchuria, the ancestral homeland of the non-Han Manchu people who ruled the Qing dynasty. This plague took a form unfamiliar to many medical practitioners at the time. Instead of the bubonic type, which required physical contact for infection, this version was pneumonic: it could be transmitted through the air. In this form, it spread quickly through population centres and along railways. Historians and anthropologists have studied this epidemic crisis as a landmark moment in which Western biomedicine gained authority among Chinese policymakers; it also provided an opportunity for Japan and Russia to expand their colonial influence in the region via strategic medical charity (Gamsa 2006; Summers 2012; Lynteris 2014). The Qing government invited Wu Liande (伍連德), a Penang-born, Cambridge-trained physician and then director of the Imperial Army Medical College, to travel to Manchuria to investigate the situation. His interventions included strict isolation of cases, laboratory tests, extensive disinfection, use of personal protective equipment by trained medical workers, and mass cremation of victims (Wu 1959, 1, 23–32). In short, these practices asserted the authority of Euro–American biomedicine in China – and, in Wu's view, the incompetence of practitioners of Chinese medicine. 'The native practitioners as a rule entertained wrong ideas of the cause of pneumonic plague', decried Wu, whereas 'The highly satisfactory results achieved by the modern-trained anti-plague staff ... gave a great fillip [stimulus] to scientific medical practice throughout China' (Wu 1959, 37). Yet this ostensible success of Western medicine did not actually employ effective novel therapeutic measures against the disease. Its success relied instead upon placing infected cases in restrictive quarantines (Lei 2010), thus terrifying local people (Gamsa 2006, 156–63).

The outbreak had significant consequences for international health. After the perceived success of Wu Liande's mission, the Qing court convened an International Plague Conference at Shenyang in April 1911. In hosting such a meeting, with a format and invitee list similar to those of the International Sanitary Conferences, the Qing administration demonstrated the ambition and the organisational capacity to participate in networks of international health. It happened at a key moment of growth for this field, as its constituent organisations – notably the International Office of Public Health, established in 1907 – attracted funding and interest from a range of participants (Knab 2011, 88). The meeting succeeded in showcasing China as not only a place where epidemics had their origins, but also one where epidemics could be studied and resolved. Delegates from across Europe, North America, Russia, and Japan attended the conference. They borrowed laboratory spaces to do their own research and spent weeks discussing the pathology and transmission of the plague. The conference proceedings dedicated much attention to the theory that the plague was the result of zoonotic transmission, not from rats, as had been seen previously (see Figure 2), but rather from tarbagans or marmots, small local mammals which were hunted for their fur. This theory posited that although local Mongolian and Buryat hunters had learned through experience and tradition to avoid

Figure 2 'In the laboratory: searching for infected rats'. Wu 1911, 61. Use courtesy Needham Research Institute. http://www.cambridge.org/Brazeltonfigure2

potentially diseased animals, the many Chinese trappers then entering the tarbagan trade had not, making the latter the cause of the disease outbreak (Petrie 1912, 410–14). This theory, formulated by Chinese and Russian researchers working together, was questioned extensively in the years following the conference (Lynteris 2019, 67).

Nonetheless, the conference provided important opportunities for attendees to gain expertise and professional standing in the emerging field of international health. Wu Liande, above all, stood to benefit. His training and identity as an Overseas Chinese allowed him to draw on networks and resources that fostered the development of biomedicine in China, first and foremost through the International Plague Conference (Soon 2020a, 25–30). In subsequent years, Wu found himself in the role of a medical officer of public health, a career path he promoted as a respectable and growing profession for fellow physicians of Western medicine (Lei 2014, 54–5). But Wu was far from the only Chinese delegate to have profited professionally from the meeting (see Figure 3). Quan Shaoqing (全紹清, also Ch'uan Shao-ching), at the time a professor at the Imperial Medical College, went on to complete graduate work at the Harvard School of Public Health in the 1920s; he eventually became director of the National Epidemic Prevention Bureau (see Section 1.3), Army Medical College in Beijing, and, later, the head of Tianjin's municipal health department

Figure 3 Delegates of the International Plague Conference in Session.
Dr Wu Lien-teh (President) with Professor S. Kitasato on his left
(top of the table). From Wu 1934, 472; image courtesy Wellcome Collection and
Cambridge Digital Library.

(Rogaski 2004, 234; Bu 2017, 119). Wu and Quan provide just two examples. More generally, we will see that a small group of highly trained and experienced individuals dominated health administration in China in the decades following 1910, and the Manchurian plague proved vital to the forging of their careers.

The International Plague Conference provided a foundation for subsequent Chinese participation in international health organisations. Shortly after its conclusion, China sent Lim Boon Keng (林文慶, also Lin Wenqing) as a delegate to the International Sanitary Conference in Paris, which ran from November 1911 to January 1912. Lim – a member of the Overseas Chinese trained at Edinburgh and a prominent physician in his native Singapore – was attending as director of what the Conference described as the Institute of Public Health in Beijing, but what might be better described as the Department of Health in the Ministry of Internal Affairs (Ministère des Affaires Étrangères 1912, 13; Soon 2014, 27, 32).

At the Paris conference, Lim gave a speech pushing back against the notion that China totally lacked public health, explaining that 'in China, a hygienic regime has been instituted for a long time, but until these past few years, it was inspired by very ancient methods and did not have the better experience of science' (Ministère des Affaires Étrangères 1912, 47). Lim explained that in recent years, the Qing state had embraced modern (and biopolitical) ideas of public health, but that its plans required time to implement. The plan was for the state to establish a 'perfected sanitary service' in a major city, then use it to train an elite corps of technical personnel who would then be distributed across other cities to train subsidiary technicians. Lim then turned to the diseases whose control preoccupied the attention of the Conference. 'The plague', Lim claimed, 'propagates itself, in general, from India to China; the localities in which it breaks out are well known to the Powers … My government, despite all difficulties, has taken all repressive measures against this disease; it has died in no time. It is easy to prevent it' (Ministère des Affaires Étrangères 1912, 47). This statement asserted Chinese competence in the face of foreign germs' invasion. It also attempted to draw attention away from the Manchurian plague event, still fresh in the minds of many, by invoking the fear of epidemic danger from elsewhere.

Yet the sunny future of Chinese public health that Lim presented was a precarious one. Even as he spoke, revolution was fomenting, and the ability of any Chinese state to provide hygienic services was very much in question. Lim's comments nonetheless spoke to transformations that had already taken place with respect to China's place in communities of international health. For a Chinese delegate and medical expert to contribute observations and analyses of the spread of infectious disease at an International Sanitary Conference, following the successful execution of an international conference on epidemiology, demonstrated the growing significance of Chinese participation in global health decision-making.

1.3 Revolutionary Medicine: Education and Institutions

Throughout the Paris meeting, the question of who, and what government, Lim was actually representing was up for grabs. On 10 October 1911, rebellion broke out against the Qing empire with the Wuchang Uprising in Hubei province. By 1 November – just days before the International Sanitary Conference convened – Yuan Shikai (袁世凱) had been appointed president of a new Republic of China. Indeed, Lim ended his speech by saying, 'Now, as the new Cabinet of Peking is not yet definitively constituted due to current events in China, I may follow the work of the Conference with you, but I may not take any decisions on its adherence to the International Convention. The decision of my Government will be communicated to you later through diplomatic channels' (Ministère des Affaires Étrangères 1912, 48). In other words, Lim's authority was limited by uncertainties over who actually held power in Beijing.

The revolution had lasting consequences for public health in China and for how Chinese people connected with foreign states in sanitary cooperation. By 1911, physicians trained in Western medicine found themselves in one of two broad groups by virtue of their education. On the one hand was an elite group trained in the Anglo-American tradition, which emphasised study in independent universities and research institutes; on the other hand was the much larger number who had studied in Japan following the German–Japanese statist approach. Adopting precedents first set by Rudolf Virchow in Prussia, then Gotō Shinpei (後藤 新平) in Japan, the latter tradition promoted sanitary policing and sanitation as a responsibility of the national government: in other words, the straightforward exertion of biopower as an ideal. In 1912, the physician-statesman Tang Erhe (湯爾和) established the National Medical College in Beijing. This school trained graduates in a Western medical curriculum modelled on Japanese precedents, and Tang recruited faculty from Japanese and Japanese-trained Chinese physicians. Historians have argued that this educational model produced 'a particular way of globalizing Western scientific medicine, one that resulted from Chinese engagements with Japan's earlier appropriation and improvisation of German models of medical education, reorganized yet again to suit the needs of Republican China' (Luesink and Asen 2019, 90).

This approach, with its strong emphasis on state support for medicine, contrasted with the Anglo-American tradition, whose alumni ironically tended to hold more state power by virtue of their elite status. In 1915, a group of graduates, mostly from British and American medical schools, formed the National Medical Association of China. They counted among their ranks Wu Liande and Yan Fuqing (顏福慶), who organised a public health committee within the Association; they also advocated for health education and infectious disease control, as well as the establishment of a national health administration (Chen 1989, 26–7). This group worked cooperatively with missionary medical endeavours to form a Joint Council on Public Health devoted to the development and execution of urban health campaigns. These operations, carried out in over twelve major Chinese cities between 1915 and 1916, mobilised local administrations and elites to promote public health using public lectures, exhibitions, and displays of lantern slides or films. The programmes indicated China's participation in a 'global phenomenon' of public health campaigns that swept Europe and North America in the same decades; to the aims of social reform that motivated campaigns in those places, Chinese organisers added westernising, modernising goals (Bu 2009, 305–14).

Although the two schools of Western medical training prevalent in China during the 1910s diverged in many ways, their members were united in two goals: contributing to the new Republic's efforts to control epidemics; and publicising those efforts to the world. The 1910 outbreak was just one episode in a longer stream of infectious diseases to strike north-east China. In its aftermath, Wu Liande established the North Manchurian Plague Prevention Service as a permanent government bureau to oversee epidemic control in the region. After the fall of the Qing, the Chinese Maritime Customs Service agreed to fund Wu's new bureau (Soon 2020a, 31). Subsequent events justified this investment, as a series of epidemics struck north China during the 1910s and 1920s. A cholera outbreak in 1919 was particularly severe, as was a second pneumonic plague event in 1920–1 (Wu and Chun 1922, 182, 1922b, 4). Over the following two decades, the Service established urban medical infrastructures across north-east China that provided health care to animal as well as human patients, conducted laboratory examinations, and supported medical education. Wu more generally served as an ambassador for Chinese public health abroad, presenting research at conferences and publishing it in Euro–American medical journals (Soon 2020a, 32–4). Chinese participation in international health projects extended beyond the missions of individual delegates. In 1908, health administrators, doctors, and other experts across East Asia established the Far Eastern Association of Tropical Medicine in Manila as an intergovernmental (largely inter-colonial) organisation for medical cooperation that could address specific regional concerns that were unrecognised by the International Sanitary Conferences. Between 1910 and

1938, it held ten conferences with representatives from polities spanning Asia and approved resolutions for quarantine cooperation and multinational public health campaigns (Akami 2016).

Growing regional and global integration of public health reporting grew more pressing with the emergence of new epidemic outbreaks. In 1918 an influenza pandemic caused by the subtype H1N1 spread around the world in the aftermath of the First World War. The medical reports of the Chinese Maritime Customs Service offer a means of surveying the extent of the pandemic's impact on China in descriptive terms; they suggest that it spread to some major eastern cities and caused substantial morbidity and mortality there. In Shanghai, tram cars were disinfected every night in order to prevent a major outbreak (Iijima 2003, 105–6). Just a year after the emergence of the influenza pandemic, two institutions were established that would have significant consequences for public health in China. The first, the National Epidemic Prevention Bureau, was founded to prevent and control infectious diseases. At first, the Bureau's remit, as covered by its first offices at the Temple of Heaven in Beijing, was limited to north China. Its primary responsibility was the development of vaccines and sera against smallpox, plague, and other infectious diseases. Its staff also collected epidemiological information, conducted urban vaccination and public health campaigns, and supported microbiological research. Over the 1920s, the Bureau expanded and established offices across the Republic of China. Its employees came to participate in domestic and international networks of biomedical research, forming new connections between public health activities and emerging disciplines of microbiology (Brazelton 2019, 23–7).

The second institution founded in 1919, Peking Union Medical College (PUMC), is more famous. In 1914, the Rockefeller Foundation had surveyed social conditions across the country and concluded that China needed significant long-term investment – but public health was not a priority for its envisioned work (Lei 2014, 55–6). The Foundation therefore focused its efforts in China not on hygiene, but medical education – although we will see that the medical teaching staff it hired eventually played key roles in the promotion of public health. In 1919, the Rockefeller Foundation and its China Medical Board founded PUMC with the goal of training an elite student body in cutting-edge methods and practices of biomedicine. It soon became known as the 'Johns Hopkins of China'. The lengthy curriculum, taught in English, included laboratory science and extensive clinical training. The College was the only school of medicine that the Rockefeller Foundation ever established and administered directly; by 1931 it had invested more money in China than any country outside the United States, largely through PUMC (Bullock 1980, 33–43; Basch 1999, 47; Litsios 2005, 297).

The first decades of the twentieth century saw rapid transformation of public health in China – and increasing involvement with international and global health discourses and organisations. The Manchurian plague in 1910–11 created a crisis of epidemic management. Yet it also created novel opportunities for individuals like Wu Liande to win professional victories over competing medical traditions, as well as advance their research careers and the field of epidemiology. The Manchurian event also offered a means for the Qing dynasty to assert competence in epidemic management and interest in international health collaboration. After the fall of the Qing, the 1911 revolution opened new possibilities for medical experts and administrators seeking to exert biopower. New public health institutions arose, and Chinese delegates participated in new medical organisations that crossed national borders. Yet epidemic diseases continued to afflict much of China's population. Although the Republican state supported health projects, its authority was limited and many Chinese territories were in reality governed by regional warlords. In the 1920s a new political party, the Nationalists, began amassing power; under its auspices, China would embark on ambitious projects of public and international health.

2 The World's Laboratory

This section explores how transnational projects in China led to the formulation of distinctive strategies of public health. In the 1920s and 1930s, China provided an experimental space for the Rockefeller Foundation and the League of Nations Health Organization (LNHO) to build new kinds of expertise. In China, these agencies tested methods of 'social medicine', which took seriously the social determinants of health (Packard 2016, 72). However, the application of a social approach to public health in China during the zenith of the Nationalist Party's power from 1927 to 1937 failed to realise a workable national health strategy. Meanwhile, doctors of Chinese medicine reformulated their profession to survive and compete with critics who advocated for their wholesale replacement with Western biomedicine. Japan's invasion of China in 1937 did not mark the end of transnational organisations' investments in Chinese health projects. Instead, these groups moved their biopolitical attentions to the country's interior, where both epidemiological dangers and the needs of local populations were even greater than the field sites in eastern China that had previously captured their interest.

2.1 Experimenting with Ideals of Social and State Medicine

In the 1920s, two major agencies, one intergovernmental and one philanthropic, made China a target of their benevolence. The League of Nations became involved in public health early in its institutional existence. The League established an Epidemic Commission in 1920, which eventually became a formal Health Organization (LNHO) in 1924. The Organization's leaders broadly endorsed views of social medicine, a concept formulated by Rudolf Virchow and other nineteenth-century European social reformers that defined 'health' as a state meeting basic socio-political as well as hygienic standards (Porter and Porter 1988, 94–5; Anderson, Smith, and Sidel 2005, 28). As we will see, social medicine broadly appealed to medical administrators in China.

One of the first projects LNHO undertook was the 1925 establishment of a Far Eastern Bureau in Singapore which served as a regional centre for epidemiological intelligence. Building on the precedent set by the Far Eastern Association of Tropical Medicine, the Bureau relied on wireless telegraph networks – and Rockefeller Foundation funding – to coordinate and disseminate information about epidemics in the region (Manderson 2009; Akami 2016). In the same year, LNHO's medical director, Ludwik Rajchman, travelled to China and soon became personally invested in the development of public health infrastructure in the Republic of China. Rajchman had studied bacteriology at the Pasteur Institute and, after contributing to anti-typhus work in his native Poland in the aftermath of the First World War, was appointed Director of the League's Epidemic Commission in 1920 (Balińska 1991, 457–9). When Rajchman first visited China in 1925, he was struck by its lack of health infrastructure, particularly the absence of a nationally coordinated port quarantine service. Following the Nationalist Party's 1927 consolidation of power, Rajchman accepted an invitation to sit on an International Advisory Council for a new Ministry of Health (Borowy 2009b, 206–7; Bu 2017, 163).

Rajchman was not the only foreigner drawn to the project of public health in China who exerted an outsized influence on the field. John B. Grant joined PUMC as its new professor of public health in 1921. The son of a Canadian medical missionary, Grant had grown up in the coastal city of Ningbo before attending medical school at the University of Michigan. His route back to China was a circuitous one, established through employment with the International Health Board of the Rockefeller Foundation. Grant was first assigned to hygiene initiatives in North Carolina, then hookworm surveying in China; these early experiences led him to the conclusion that – contrary to the Foundation's strategies at the time – public health work in China should incorporate broad educational efforts, model programmes for widespread emulation, and lobbying for legal institutions of hygiene (Bullock 1980, 135–9; Bu 2017, 118).

Reflecting these values, Grant opened a Health Demonstration Station in an inner ward of Beijing in 1925. The Station co-opted public authority and budgets to serve the health of this ward's 58,000 residents. In charge of the staff, which included six doctors and seventeen nurses drawn mostly from the National Epidemic Prevention Bureau, was a Japanese-trained physician, Fang Shisan (方石珊, also Fang Qing 方擎). The Station thus represented a productive union of those trained in Anglo-American and German–Japanese approaches. Its activities included gathering vital statistics, making it, along with the Bureau, an important early force in the amassing of epidemiological data. It also provided health services to a local factory and schools, and ran prenatal and paediatric clinics. By 1926, all PUMC students were required to complete a clerkship at the Station (Bullock 1980, 145–9; Bu 2017, 119–22). Former student C. C. Chen (陳志潛, also Chen Zhiqian) wrote of Grant's pedagogy: 'For many students, the face-to-face exposure to the suffering of clinical patients and their increasing awareness of the health problems of millions of Chinese men, women, and children in the countryside was a shocking experience . . . the critical relationship of public health to national renewal became increasingly clear' (Chen 1989, 25). The experiences of the Station participants led them to conclude that the system most appropriate for China was state medicine, an approach that fit within the broad framework of social medicine but which was distinct in its allocation of responsibility for health to national governments.

Grant recommended the implementation of such a system at a transformative moment for China. In 1927 the Nationalist Party, led by the militarist Chiang Kai-shek (蔣介石), consolidated power over much of central and eastern China. Seeing an opportunity to promote the cause of public health in China at a critical moment of governmental restructuring, Grant wrote a memorandum to Party leaders encouraging the establishment of a government agency dedicated to public health. Citing the recent examples of Great Britain and the Soviet Union, Grant suggested that a Ministry of Health should take full control of all health services in the country. Although many of these points were erased or altered in the Chinese translation of the memorandum, a Ministry of Health was indeed established in 1928 (Lei 2014, 60–5).

The Ministry's inauguration promised fulfilment of the aims of state medicine. Grant immediately sought to build bridges between the new Ministry and LNHO as a means to further lessen divides between professional groups trained in the Anglo-American versus German–Japanese traditions. In this, Rajchman was a key ally. In 1931, the League of Nations initiated an extensive programme of technical cooperation with China. Rajchman and a group of three other experts all came to China as consultants to the Ministry of Health (Bullock 1980, 154–5). Between 1931 and 1934, they provided support for the (newly renamed) National Health Administration's establishment of a Central Health Service. The project set up a Central Field Health Station and Central Hospital in Nanjing, built quarantine facilities, and trained quarantine officers (Rajchman 1934: 57–8).

These initiatives were founded as pilot programmes to serve as strong foundations and centres for national health work – the term Rajchman used was 'nucleus' (Rajchman 1934, 57) – but ultimately they served as an experimental site for the ideological goals of LNHO. It was through these projects in China that Rajchman worked out the ambitions of LNHO to create transferable 'blueprints' for national health systems and to promote a single concept of health which had socio-political aspects as well as medical meanings (Borowy 2009a, 312). Rajchman's biographer has claimed that it was he who first coined the term 'technical assistance' as a concept according to which the wealthier nations of the world might provide scientific and technological materials, training, and funding to poorer ones (Balińska 1991, 459). The project thus held lasting significance insofar as it provided a model for international aid to what became known as 'developing countries' after the Second World War, giving new life to Western civilising missions in a post-colonial political order. It also made Rajchman a canonical 'international expert' in an emerging paradigm in which expertise was transferable to a variety of non-Western settings (Zanasi 2007).

2.2 Chinese Administrators as Partners in Health

Although Rajchman and Grant were influential figures, Chinese physicians and health administrators were not passive recipients of foreign aid. They actively campaigned for foreign investment in projects deemed important to the Nationalist state, and which reflected values held widely by Chinese intellectuals of the time. And they perceived Western philanthropic and diplomatic organisations as part of a broader spectrum of potential partners. For instance, Chinese physicians also explored participation in socialist networks of health. The Soviet Union's Commissariat of Public Health had been established with the goal of offering free health care to all citizens, with the understanding that health and disease could be shaped by social causes. Over the 1920s, numerous bilateral initiatives sought to promote this approach to public health (Solomon 2017, 194). In 1934, a two-part article in the *Chinese Medical Journal* discussed 'the essence of Soviet public health' (Jiang 1934a, 1934b). The author, Jiang Taosheng (江濤聲), had studied medicine in Berlin and joined the Communist Party there in 1931 (Guo 1993, 295). Jiang surveyed public health in the Soviet Union, including vital statistics, the state of hygienic programmes and infrastructures, and medical education. He claimed that 'in the establishment of experimental biology research and social hygiene, [Soviet medicine] has surpassed most European and American states in development' (Jiang 1934a, 1393). However, a 1935 visit to Moscow, Leningrad, and Kiev left C. C. Chen less than impressed. He reported to LNHO that he thought the Soviet

Union 'was ahead of many countries in practicing state medicine, but the quality of its service had to be improved' (Chen 1989, 102).

Chen exemplified the kind of professional who benefited from the Nationalist Party's ascent to power: an elite PUMC graduate, he was in a strong position to make decisions about future directions in international health on China's behalf. Indeed, Chen assumed authority over a key new public health project in the Nationalist state. Ding County, in Hebei province, became the site of an experiment in scientific management that would provide a lasting model for international health. In 1926, a local activist invited China's Mass Education Movement to establish their headquarters in the county (Merkel-Hess 2016, 26). Originally a non-governmental initiative to promote mass literacy, the Movement sought to achieve educational, agricultural, public health, and political modernising reforms in a way that did not simply impose Western norms but instead responded to local conditions (Schmalzer 2002, 3). Its leader, Y. C. James Yen (晏陽初, also Yan Yangchu), was keen to enlist PUMC graduates to promulgate scientific medicine in Ding County, and in the late 1920s he recruited Grant as an advisor (Litsios 2005, 300).

In 1932, Chen became Ding County's director of Public Health on the grounds that 'the health project in itself was quite insignificant. If the model could be used for training, however, I felt that its impact on rural inhabitants could be very great' (Chen 1989, 71). Chen established formal connections between the Movement and PUMC, so that medical students completed field studies there and the PUMC hospital offered services to residents of Ding County. He also recruited medical staff from the Hunan-Yale (Xiangya) Medical College in Changsha and the provincial medical schools of Hunan and Hebei provinces (Chen 1936, 79). Chen organised a survey of local health conditions and resources, and then developed a medical infrastructure that integrated health services across three administrative levels of district, sub-district, and village. He also planned a system for training village health workers in basic clinical care and disease prevention. Their responsibilities included the vaccination of villagers against smallpox (see Figure 4), construction of sanitary toilet infrastructures, pest control, and experiments with birth control and the retraining of midwives (Merkel-Hess 2016, 30–1). Chen admitted the ad hoc nature of these programmes, writing, 'I had no idea what might or might not be practical; thus, our ideas evolved as we went along' (Chen 1989, 76–8). He envisioned his work as helping China to meet a standard of medical and preventive care that would place it on par with developed nations. For example, he began a 1936 report on maternal and child health measures in Ding County by writing, 'Before people begin to appreciate the importance of mothers and children in relation to the welfare of the nation and before the community is rich and intelligent enough to seek technical assistance, it is difficult to expect rapid

RURAL China is a virgin field for the application of modern medicine and public health.

Figure 4 This photo appeared in a report on Ding County published by the Milbank Memorial Fund, one of the supporters of the project. A Rural Health Experiment in China 1930, 108.

growth of maternity and child health activities' (Chen 1936, 75). In other words, supporting maternal and infant health offered a means for China to demonstrate its competence in comparison with other 'rich and intelligent' peoples of the world (Johnson 2011, xxi–xxii).

Ding County was not just an experimental site for working out new approaches to public health. It was also a showcase for these approaches that enabled Chen and other leaders of the Movement to enlist foreign allies and investment. Visitors from abroad included Selskar Gunn, the Rockefeller Foundation's vice president for Europe, and Andrija Štampar, an outspoken advocate for social medicine and an active member of LNHO (Chen 1989, 100).

Ding County brought together Gunn and Grant, who cooperated to develop a new project of health intervention in China under the Rockefeller Foundation's auspices. The Foundation's International Health Division was the main agency through which it effected interventions to export American tropical medicine and implement top-down technical methods for disease prevention around the world (Palmer 2010). Yet the Foundation's China Program, led by Štampar and Gunn with input from Grant between 1935 and 1937, diverged from the Division's characteristically top-down and highly technical approach by virtue of its highly interdisciplinary nature. The goal of the China Program was to establish a new society in which social scientists conducted nation-building projects (Litsios 2005). In 1935, Grant explained in a memo,

> In medicine ... the problem of prime importance would be that of organiza-
> tion and methods of medical protection *as a whole*. It is believed that an attack
> in the medical field conceived on such lines would ultimately be more
> effective in dealing with such individual problems as hookworm and malaria
> and their control, than have been the specific efforts in the past for their
> solution. (Grant 1935, 2, emphasis added)

At Ding County, the China Program supported public health alongside a range of training programmes in sanitary engineering, agriculture, and economics (Bullock 1980, 159). Medicine thus represented one disciplinary strand in a bigger project. 'Indeed there is a sense in which China might become a vast laboratory in the social sciences, with implications that would be international in scope', read a report from a Foundation committee meeting approving the programme (Rockefeller Foundation 1934, 105). These grand ambitions were ultimately hamstrung by the 1937 outbreak of war.

The impact of the Ding County model was felt far and wide. For instance, in March 1937, Harry Gear, a public health officer in Pretoria, discussed the county as a model for South Africa (Gear 1937, 153). Between 1932 and 1935, Gear had worked at the newly opened Henry Lester Institute of Technical Education in Shanghai as head of its Department of Preventive Medicine (Dr. H.S. Gear 1961, 465; Marks 2014, 176). Although not a medical school, the Institute competed with PUMC for prestige and recognition as an institute sponsoring biomedical research (Fu 2016, 272–9). Gear returned to South Africa inspired to apply the Ding County model to local surroundings. He claimed in 1937 that Chen's work betrayed 'an attitude which would be useful towards our non-European populations. Experimental areas in our native terri-tories ... would be veritable gold mines in the useful direction and demonstra-tion given to solution of all native problems' (Gear 1937, 154). The identification of China's experience as relevant to South Africa revealed

characteristic assumptions of racial hierarchy in which non-European populations provided targets for European intervention. Gear's subsequent promotion
of social medicine based on the Ding County model was 'in many ways crucial'
to the establishment of a community health centre at Pholela which became an
explicit model for South African health systems (Marks 2014, 176). Gear was
later appointed as an assistant director-general of the WHO between 1951 and
1958, and as secretary-general of the World Medical Association in 1961 (Dr.
H.S. Gear 1961, 465).

Although the bulk of power and money in international health remained with
institutions based in the so-called Global North – and it was therefore essential
to gain the allyship of organisations like the Rockefeller Foundation or League
of Nations – Chinese physicians and health administrators like C. C. Chen acted
with the interests of their own country in mind. Ding County provided a model
experimental setting – proof of concept, perhaps, for the Rockefeller
Foundation's vision of China as a 'vast laboratory' – where officials and
intellectuals could indicate the extent of their ambitions to potential funders,
but it was far from the only site of new public health endeavours during the
Nanjing Decade. The range of projects during this period reflected ongoing
commitments not just to social medicine, but also to involvement in international health. Yet the pursuit of these programmes in the Chinese context
revealed the potential limits of the application of those ideals.

2.3 International Health in Service of Scientific Nationalism

Why were Chinese administrators so open to the interventions of Rajchman,
Grant, Gunn, and others? The Nanjing Decade between 1927 and 1937 was a
period of remarkable *scientism*, in which science was valorised as an end to
itself – and the means by which China would find national strength and success
as the basis for a new value system. This ideology shaped the kinds of internationalism that Chinese intellectuals endorsed, and it made the techno-scien-
tific solutions to health problems that the League and the Rockefeller
Foundation offered particularly attractive. As the idealistic statements of C.
C. Chen suggest, many physicians and health administrators believed that their
work was the key to making China a strong, modern country. The idea that
adopting Western science would modernise and save the Chinese nation was
made especially popular by social movements of the period, like the May Fourth
Movement of 1919 which advocated strongly for the adoption of modern
science and democracy. It led a significant number of Chinese intellectuals to
advocate for changes in medical policies: specifically, the abolition of traditional medicine, the implementation of eugenics, and the establishment of a

modern health system to conform to the ideals of what they perceived as a new, global scientific medicine. Yet the challenges that Chinese medical experts encountered in pursuing these goals suggested that it might be necessary to selectively appropriate reigning international health paradigms, rather than adopt them wholesale, to meet China's particular health needs.

A corollary of scientism's valorisation of modern, Western disciplines of knowledge was the identification of deficiency in Chinese knowledge traditions; its advocates therefore targeted these perceived flaws – most infamously by attempting to abolish traditional medicine. Throughout the nineteenth and early twentieth centuries, Chinese medical practices and theories had coexisted alongside the introduction of novel anatomical, therapeutic, and preventive practices from Europe and North America (Lei 2014, 4). With the advent of Nationalist power, though, this state of affairs changed. In 1929, the Nationalist state held the first National Hygiene Conference. Physicians trained in the Western tradition voted in favour of a proposal written by Yu Yan (余岩, also Yu Yunxiu 余云岫) to curtail and marginalise the practice of Chinese medicine. The scheme required practitioners to register with the government and to attend training sessions (Andrews 2014, 83; Lei 2014, 102). Yu Yan's efforts were part of what he considered a 'medical revolution', inspired by the work of Rudolf Virchow, to seek integration of medicine and the state – stemming from the same roots as the visions of social medicine ascribed to Rajchman, Grant, and their students (Lei 2014, 97–8). For Yu, though, this vision required the selective and exclusive investment of resources and state authority in Western medicine at the expense of Chinese medicine.

This act of aggression led traditional practitioners to unite and organise resistance. On 17 March 1929, they held a protest in Shanghai that launched a 'National Medicine Movement' to protect the interests of Chinese medicine (Lei 1999, 324). This movement's advocates also achieved professional reform by establishing the National Federation of Medical and Pharmaceutical Associations, which brought together associations of Chinese medicine practitioners, pharmacists, and medicine suppliers. In 1930, the Federation was replaced by an Institute of National Medicine, funded by the Nationalist state with the remit to establish and administer hospitals and training centres, but also a mission to 'scientise' Chinese medicine (Lei 2014, 117). By 1932, the Institute oversaw an international network with over 500 member organisations in China, Hong Kong, Singapore, and the Philippines (Lei 2014, 108).

These conflicts also led practitioners of Chinese medicine to carry out epistemic reforms of the theories and practices defining their work, which ultimately made possible the emergence of a systematised 'Traditional Chinese Medicine' (TCM) later in the twentieth century (Lei 2014, 5).

New schools of Chinese medicine were established and new textbooks and journals dedicated to the field were published; in practice, these new institutions largely sought to standardise, modernise, and scientise Chinese medicine, often by excluding 'superstitious' or religious practices like geomancy or fortune-telling, as well as the medical knowledge and practices of ethnic minorities (Andrews 2014, 170–83; Farquhar and Lai 2021, 73–4).

Meanwhile, scientistic intellectuals of the Nanjing Decade did not only target Chinese medicine per se. Therapeutic theories and practices were just one part of a broader constellation of evils they associated with Chinese tradition. In the May Fourth Movement, for example, young reformers identified traditionally large, multigenerational family structures as a source of social degeneration. This assertion had a history: China had long played a significant if ambiguous role in global debates over population. From the early twentieth century, 'neo-Malthusian' economists, scientists, physicians, and feminists had constructed world overpopulation as a social, political, and economic problem, combining eugenic beliefs with emerging ecological methods (Bashford 2018, 506–7). Within these debates, China became a target of critique. Foreign demographers, economists, and other commentators claimed that it was overpopulated to the point of debilitating poverty; smaller, nuclear families would improve the nation's race and environment. The scholar Pan Guangdan (潘光旦) translated and introduced a number of eugenic discourses to Chinese audiences in the 1920s and 1930s, encouraging policies that would keep 'less desirable' people from reproducing and incentivise 'desirable' people to have more children. In other words, eugenics provided an ostensible solution to 'the problem of Chinese national character in the terrain of public health' (Chung 2010, 261, 2014). Yet policymakers did not institutionalise eugenic ideas despite significant support, in part because Sun Yat-sen (孫中山), the founding father of the Republic and a trained physician himself, had been firmly pronatalist. It was female gynaecologists, instead, who most ardently tried to implement eugenic principles by establishing birth control clinics from 1925 onwards; yet these efforts remained limited to urban centres in Beijing, Nanjing, and Shanghai (David 2018).

If scientism led its advocates to denigrate traditional Chinese medicine and family structures in the name of public health, it found more positive expression in supporting the establishment of a national health infrastructure. A variety of new institutions and organisations proliferated during the Nanjing Decade, demonstrating that public health was a key part of the nation-building project for the Nationalist Party, and that state administrators saw it as a means to transform and modernise China. In short, they endorsed visions of social medicine (Yip 1995, 35, 41). Yet the capacity of the Nationalist regime to actually deliver those visions fell short of its officials' desires.

Over the Nanjing Decade, this tension between vision and execution became more evident. Numerous agencies were set up in the years following the 1928 establishment of the Ministry of Health (renamed the National Health Administration in 1931). The Central Field Health Station mentioned above provided a driving force in establishing provincial and local health care bureaus. It also hosted a Department of Health Education which prepared popular books, pamphlets, short films, broadcasts, lectures, and lantern shows for free mass distribution across the country (see Figure 5). Between 1928 and 1931 the Ministry established a Central Hospital in Nanjing, a National Quarantine Service under Wu Liande, a Commission on Industrial Health, the First National Midwifery School, a Child Health Institute, and a Committee on School Health, followed by a Central School Health Service. These organisations planned a dazzling variety of health initiatives, from the retraining of midwives in modern sanitary childbirth practices to physical education in schools. Yet popular education activities rarely penetrated areas outside population centres, not least because they encountered conflicts with practitioners of traditional medicine. The burden of enforcing new health regulations fell on local administrations that had extremely variable relationships to the central government, and activities focusing on technical projects – following the American influence on public health in China – tended to swallow up large amounts of an already paltry budget (Yip 1995, 55–8, 62–5, 102–30). In other words, governmental health projects revealed the considerable gap between the desire for science to solve national problems and the manifestation of programmes that could deliver such solutions, especially in the countryside.

Although LNHO had played a formative role in laying the groundwork for Chinese approaches to public and especially rural health in the Nanjing Decade, it eventually found itself in an awkward position in Asia as a number of polities asserted diverging views on health needs. The 1937 Bandung Conference on Rural Hygiene, for instance, was heralded as an event that would support LNHO's efforts to identify and improve social determinants of health in Asian settings (Brown and Fee 2008, 42). Chinese delegates played a key role in the meeting; C. C. Chen and Zhang Fuliang (张福良) provided reports on Ding County, as well as coordination between public health organisations and agricultural, educational, and economic groups (Litsios 2014, 118–19). Reports associated with the conference stressed the need for local collaboration and sensitivity to indigenous languages and cultures, and conference delegates asserted the inability of Western biomedical models to be straightforwardly transposed to Asia (Borowy 2009a, 355). Although these recommendations raised new questions about the role played by LNHO and other international health organisations in East Asia, they resulted in few clear policy

Figure 5 A print worker holding up a smallpox vaccination poster beside a large printing machine, Shanghai, *c.*1933. Image courtesy of Adrienne Livesey, Elaine Ryder, Irene Brien, and Special Collections, University of Bristol Library (www.hpcbristol.net).

consequences, largely because of the outbreak of war in the Pacific (Guénel 2012, 62, 73).

2.4 Laboratory Life in the Wartime Hinterland

In July 1937, war erupted in East Asia. On the 7th, an exchange of fire between Chinese troops and Japanese soldiers outside Beijing slipped into all-out combat. By the 28th, the city had fallen and the Japanese Imperial Army cut its way southward, taking Shanghai in late October and the capital Nanjing in December. In the face of full-blown invasion, the Republican government retreated into China's interior, transferring key staffers and apparatus to Wuhan and then further up the Yangzi River. By 1938, the wartime capital of China had been established at Chongqing: a muggy, craggy, suddenly crowded city then part of Sichuan province in the south-west.

Chinese public health moved south-west, too. If in the preceding decade the Nationalist government had articulated grand modernising ambitions to establish hygienic infrastructure, during the war it confronted the limits of those ambitions – and the persistent risk of epidemic danger – in the western interior. The National Health Administration transferred to a suburb of Chongqing, where wartime public health work placed women in central roles (Barnes 2018). The National Epidemic Prevention Bureau moved its headquarters to Kunming, provincial capital of Yunnan, south of Chongqing. In the new geography of war, peripheral sites became newly prominent nodes in wartime networks of epidemic control. For instance, the Lanzhou branch of the National Epidemic Prevention Bureau, which had previously focused its efforts on the control of veterinary diseases, was renamed the National Northwest Epidemic Prevention Bureau and redirected much of its work to the manufacturing of human vaccines and sera to prevent epidemics among soldiers and refugees. The Lanzhou Bureau's extensive stables became vital national resources, since producing the vaccines that prevented human diseases like plague, cholera, and smallpox required serial passage of experimental bacterial and viral strains through live rodents, rabbits, horses, and calves (see Figure 6).

The retreat to the interior made western China a target not only for Japanese air raids, but also for transnational epidemic control efforts. If in the 1920s and early 1930s China had been the focus of interventionist projects to engage an agrarian state government in public health work, now, in wartime, it became a testing ground for novel connections between laboratory research, health administration, and material supply circulation. The LNHO sent three epidemic commissions to assist the National Health Administration in 1937 and 1938. The teams worked with local health agencies to provide immunisation and other

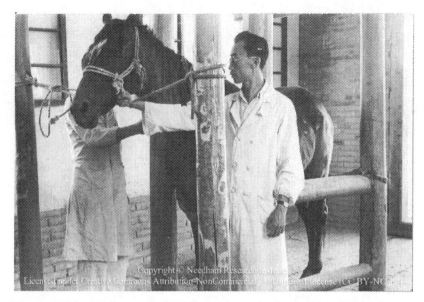

Figure 6 'A horse about to be bled for serum at the farm of the NWEPB/North-West Epidemic Prevention Bureau Vaccine Production Institute, Lanchow, Kansu'. Photo by Gordon Sanders (NRI2/10/1/1/8/5/21); image courtesy Needham Research Institute.

public health work. Back in Geneva, in 1938, LNHO administrators coordinated a cholera vaccine donation programme that shipped over 8 million doses of vaccines from nations across the world to China (Brazelton 2019, 58–65). Several international organisations sponsored the continuation of medical research in China despite its invasion, notably the Rockefeller Foundation, which sponsored research trips abroad for Chinese biologists and continued its China Program even as the participants transferred thousands of miles to the south-west. 'The exigencies of war are making it possible to extend further the coordination of experiments and services', described one 1938 report, optimistically. 'Thus, the work in social medicine is being incorporated with the rural training program of the National Health Administration ... The concentration of all Council activities within a small circumscribed area is rated by the Officers as highly advantageous to the practical purposes of the program – one of the blessings of war' (Rockefeller Foundation 1938, 11).

A host of other bilateral organisations joined the work of the League and the Foundation. The Sino–British Science Cooperation Office, under the direction of the Cambridge embryologist and historian of science Joseph Needham, offered a 'scientific post office' that provided Chinese researchers with up-to-date scientific literature and enabled them to publish their research in foreign journals (Mougey 2017, 97). The American Bureau for Medical Aid to China drew on the resources of the Chinese-American diaspora to provide financial assistance to Chinese health administrations, and coordinated the establishment of the first Chinese blood bank in wartime Kunming (Soon 2016). With minimal support from the central government, National Health Administration staffers used this financial aid to conduct a range of activities, from establishing highway health stations and epidemic prevention teams to collecting epidemiological data and otherwise supporting local health administrations (Watt 2014, 205–52). The Quaker Society of Friends also set up a China Convoy as part of its Friends Ambulance Unit, an organisation which provided a means for pacificists to contribute productively to the Allied cause by transporting drugs and medical supplies, as well as staffing mobile medical teams supporting the Nationalist army (Smith 1999, 249). In short, more transnational organisations than ever before were engaging with China's Republican government during this period.

The Republic was not the only regime governing Chinese peoples and their health during the war. The CCP, expelled from alliance with the Nationalists in 1927 and persecuted ever since, spent the war years based in the north-western region of Yan'an, in Shaanxi province. If south-west China offered a laboratory environment for Western health authorities cultivating a transferable, global expertise, then Yan'an provided another kind of experimental space, one for working out techniques and values of Communist governance in China. Medicine was one part of this experiment. For instance, the CCP established a hospital in 1939 that served as the centre for a nascent health system. These endeavours were given some support by international organisations, notably the China Defence League and the League of Nations (Watt 2014, 253–98). Interest in Soviet medicine also grew during the war with Japan; during the 1940s, the CCP sponsored the translation and publication of Soviet medical texts (Gao 2014, 196–7). By the end of the Second World War in 1945, practitioners of acupuncture and folk medicine in areas under CCP control had aligned themselves with its leadership and sought cooperation with Western medical doctors (Taylor 2005, 17).

Outside both the Nationalist- and Communist-controlled regions of China lay the considerable northern and eastern territories occupied by Japan. Here, public health offered a tool of imperial expansion, in which administrators sought to enforce hygiene to control local peoples and environments – yet the actual practices mandated were sometimes not so different from those imposed by previous governments (Rogaski 2004, 253–4). In the city of Tianjin, for example, Japanese medical workers inspected, vaccinated, and conducted laboratory examinations of the local population. This forceful imposition of hygienic modernity varied in degree rather than kind from previous efforts by the Nationalist state (Rogaski 2004, 273). In Manchuria, under Japanese control since 1931, a range of hygienic interventions and epidemic prevention projects were established (Shen 2015). Of course, 'epidemic prevention' could encompass a number of activities, and one unit for 'water purification and epidemic prevention' in Harbin served as a cover for experimental studies of Chinese prisoners of war that is today considered to have violated a number of ethical principles (Harris 1994; Kondō and Wang 2019). The horrors of Unit 731 remain contentious territory for Sino–Japanese relations today. Japanese wartime health administration operated differently across the various territories of the empire. For instance, Taiwan became an experimental space to test public health procedures that the Japanese Army planned to use in active military operations in South-East Asia (Liu 2009, 152–4). By war's end, as over 1.5 million fled to the island from mainland China, cholera, plague, smallpox, and malaria struck with force, and the colonial programmes the Japanese had enacted lapsed (Liu 2012).

In 1947, the Nationalist government published a constitution asserting the regime's commitment to state medicine, seeking ever more responsibility for and control over national populations (Lei 2014, 9). But the regime itself had only a tenuous grasp on the Chinese population. In that year, the Republic of China was losing a civil war to retain control of the Chinese mainland. By late 1949, its government had retreated from the capital at Nanjing once more – this time heading east instead of south-west, to the island of Taiwan. International health experts' dreams of state medicine would arguably be realised on both sides of the Taiwan Strait: but on the mainland, it was the People's Republic of China under the CCP that would take responsibility for the population's health.

3 Medical Circulations in the Cold War

After the end of the Second World War and ensuing civil war between Nationalist and Communist Parties, the new PRC resumed mainland China's function as an experimental space for transnational projects in global health – yet now, the main partners were allies and agents of the Union of Soviet Socialist Republics (USSR). In the 1950s the PRC participated in medical projects that took place within structures of socialist internationalism. After the Sino–Soviet split, Chinese administrators embarked on new initiatives of medical diplomacy in the 1960s and 1970s. They offered equipment, personnel, and resources to 'non-aligned' states in Asia and Africa to gain political capital. These programmes promoted a Chinese model of rural health, making liberal use of paraprofessional medical workers ('barefoot doctors', *chijiao yisheng*

赤腳醫生) who combined newly systematised forms of Chinese and Western medicine. Cold War interventions thus reflected both the legacies of earlier international organisations' experiments *and* domestic projects to preserve and enshrine a healing tradition distinct from the Western biomedicine that the former projects sought to promulgate. This model eventually won acclaim worldwide and contributed to the World Health Organization's adoption of 'primary health care' as a guiding principle at the end of the 1970s.

3.1 A Period of Isolation?

Chinese representatives were integral to the establishment of the World Health Organization. In April 1945, at the United Nations (UN) Conference on International Organization in San Francisco, the diplomat and physician Szeming Sze (施思明, also Shi Siming) first proposed the establishment of an organisation devoted to international health along with the Norwegian Karl Evang and Brazilian Geraldo De Paula Souza. Sze participated in a subsequent conference of UN member governments to design the new agency and argued for the name 'World Health Organization' (Sze 1982, 1–17).

Despite this promising start, in which a Chinese physician played an active role in establishing the most prominent international medical agency of the post-war era, most narratives of the history of global health between 1945 and 1965 do not devote much space to China (Packard 2016, 112–31; Cueto, Brown, and Fee 2019, 62–114). This is partly due to the transformations that overtook China itself in the years immediately following the Second World War. Shortly after Japan's surrender, the Nationalist and Communist Parties relapsed into civil war. The CCP consolidated control over the mainland in 1949, and Mao Zedong (毛泽东) announced the founding of the PRC on 1 October. But the Nationalist Party did not die so easily. Chiang Kai-shek had moved his administration and seat of power before, during the war with Japan; this time, instead of fleeing west over land, he transferred his government east over water. From the island province of Taiwan that had so recently been a colonial territory of Japan, Chiang's Republic of China continued to represent 'China' in the World Health Organization, UN, and other organisations of international governance.

China was not the only territory to undergo such bifurcation in the 1940s. Other states – Korea, Palestine, India – experienced similar rifts of governance accompanied by mass migration, border-drawing, and violence (see Figure 7). In the case of mainland China and Taiwan, schism yielded two governments that both laid claim to authority over 'one China' encompassing both territories. The result was administrative twinning: two Chinese public health administrations, two systems of medical education, and two approaches to foreign medical exchanges,

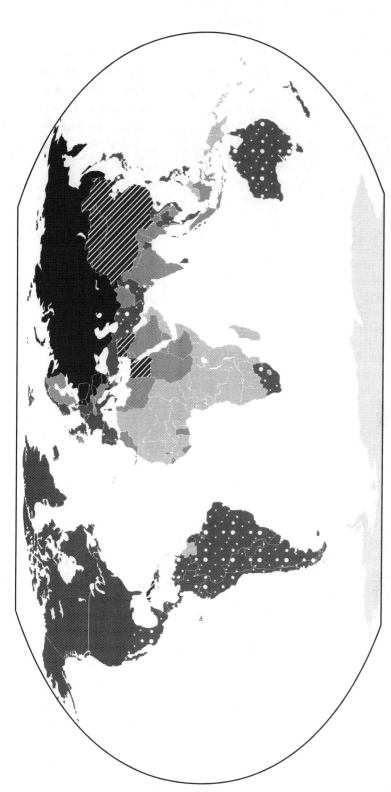

Figure 7 A map of the Cold War world in 1959. The black shading indicates Warsaw Pact member states; the diagonal stripes indicate other allies of the USSR; the dark gray indicates NATO member states; the dotted shading indicates other allies of the USA; the medium gray indicates non-aligned states; and the light gray shading indicates colonized states. Image created by Sémhur and reproduced courtesy of Creative Commons license 1.0 Generic. http://www .cambridge.org/Brazeltonfigure7

each of which ostensibly served the same total population but actually differed greatly in terms of priorities and methods of governance, external influences, and populations served. This section cannot hope to give a full accounting of that divergence, but instead focuses on its ramifications for international health. Although the PRC was absent from the WHO between 1949 and 1972, it was hardly isolated from international health. By virtue of its status as the globe's most populous country, what happened in Chinese public health mattered to the world. Furthermore, international networks bound the PRC to other socialist states and the non-aligned 'Third World'.

3.2 Pavlov in the Delivery Room: Medical Movements in the Socialist World

From 1949, the imperative to 'learn from the Soviet Union' shaped Chinese health policy and programming. As we have seen, the Soviet model of public health had aroused the interest of Chinese physicians as early as the 1930s. After the establishment of the PRC, Soviet state medicine offered a model for achieving the goal of providing accessible, comprehensive medical care to the Chinese population. It also suggested a preferable alternative to Western biomedicine, which had assumed negative political connotations in the wake of PRC–US hostilities in the Korean War (Ahn 2013, 140). Moreover, a natural environment which had created common interests in overlapping *materia medica*, as well as a shared desire for self-sufficiency in exploiting indigenous materials in pharmaceutical production, provided a firm foundation for cooperation between Soviet and Chinese forces (Chee 2021, 54–5). Over the 1950s, a substantial number of Soviet medical workers arrived in the PRC to assist in establishing new health administrations and reorganising medical education, while Chinese students travelled to Moscow to study medicine. Many of the former worked at the Soviet-funded and designed Beijing Soviet Red Cross Hospital (Gao 2014, 199–204), while Russian physicians in China studied and researched acupuncture (Su 2021, 147–8).

In China, educational reforms contributed to processes of centralisation, nationalisation, and specialisation in medicine. These trends placed greater emphasis on political and practical training, preventive interventions, and the works of Ivan Pavlov as a basis for biomedical theories. The latter took its most famous form in approaches to childbirth that deployed Pavlovian theories of conditioned response (Gao 2014, 205–9). The 'psycho-prophylactic method of delivery' or 'painless childbirth', instituted in the Soviet Union in 1951, presented Chinese policymakers with a resolution to ongoing conflicts between Euro–American, medicalised childbirth practices – identified ideologically with Western capitalism – and traditional midwifery, associated with the superstition and feudalism characteristic of China's imperial past. This method was premised on the theory that pain in conventional childbirth was a psychological, rather than physical, problem; it therefore required psychological correctives through lectures, regulated breathing, massage, and the use of pressure points. In 1952, the PRC Ministry of Health formally endorsed psycho-prophylactic delivery as a practice that all medical organisations should study and implement. However, its methods were not transferred wholesale from the Soviet Union to China. Chinese translations of Russian texts stressed radical belief in the power of the method and eschewed the non-psychological techniques, like breathing exercises or massage, that were recommended to support it. Although high success rates were reported by the clinics ordered to adopt psycho-prophylactic methods, urban hospital staff did not appear to adopt the new practice with enthusiasm, and the practice declined after the end of the Korean War in 1953 (Ahn 2013, 144–53).

Soviet influences also shaped aspects of the new Chinese medicine that was being forged in the post-1949 era, blurring the boundaries between 'Western' and 'Eastern' traditions. Another practice grouped under the rubric of Pavlovian theories, organotherapy, found footing in the PRC during the 1950s. The premise of organotherapy was that therapeutic benefits accrued from injecting solutions derived from animal tissues into the human body. An offshoot of organotherapy, histotherapy or tissue therapy, involved transplanting miniscule amounts of plant, animal, or human tissues under the skin to treat diseased parts of the body. This practice received a mandate from the PRC Ministry of Health to be taught and implemented in hospitals, medical schools, and research groups. Although it was introduced in the PRC as a Soviet practice, Soviet practitioners claimed that histotherapy had its origins in Chinese medicine and its use of animal therapies (Chee 2021, 64–7). One exemplary area of convergence was a concern with deer horn, which had long been a component in Chinese medicines, and which Soviet pharmacologists claimed contained a substance called 'pantocrin', consisting of hormones that could treat human male sexual dysfunction. The consequent mass production of pills made from deer antler velvet in the Soviet Union and China provided what Liz Chee has described as 'likely the first internationally vended modern pharmaceutical to be based on Chinese medicine, despite its Russian invention' (Chee 2021, 68).

3.3 Serving the Masses through Medical Research, Administration, and Care

Towards the end of the 1950s, relations between the PRC and the Soviet Union began to disintegrate. The installation of Nikita Khrushchev as leader of the Soviet Union following the death of Iosif Stalin displeased Mao Zedong, who remained ideologically committed to a hard-line, Stalinist opposition to Western capitalist imperialism and rapid economic development via collectivisation (Lüthi 2008, 1–2). By the time of this 'Sino–Soviet split', Soviet influence on medicine had contributed to a distinctive approach to public health in the PRC. The CCP leadership continued to invest in public health programmes to provide comprehensive care to rural villages as well as cities. These programmes varied between 1949 and the end of the Maoist era in 1978, but salient features included continuing efforts to unify Chinese and Western medical traditions, control of a range of infectious diseases thanks in large part to mass immunisation, a large-scale effort to control the parasitic disease schistosomiasis, and the evolution of schemes to train part-time paraprofessional health workers, who would come to be known as barefoot doctors. The early PRC also saw the expansion of faunal medicalisation, the process by which drugs with animal components were integrated into officially sanctioned medical practice and economic networks, just as pharmacology took on remarkable prominence within the life sciences (Chee 2021, 5, 11).

Shortly after the establishment of the PRC, its involvement in the Korean War instigated the 1952 launch of the Patriotic Hygiene Campaign, a broad programme promoting public health practices ranging from mass immunisation to street-sweeping and sanitation projects (Rogaski 2004, 285–99; see Figure 8). Separate from these programmes was a high-level, large-scale project to control one particular parasitic disease. Soon after the establishment of the PRC, the central government determined that schistosomiasis, a rural disease transmitted by snails, posed a major threat to the national military and economy, and it convened a special committee to address this disease (Gross 2016, 16–20). Although hailed as a spectacular success in government and popular accounts, prevention work largely failed, and chemical control methods implemented in the 1950s posed environmental risks to China's land and people. In the early 1960s, many anti-schistosomiasis units were dissolved as medical resources were diverted towards new epidemiological threats, commune health care collapsed, and hospitals encountered financial difficulties following the Great Leap Forward: a collectivisation project between 1958 and 1961 that resulted in severe famine (Zhou 2020, 135–47, 163–6). The crucial turning point in schistosomiasis control came later, with the 1966 onset of the Cultural Revolution, a movement in which Mao Zedong provoked radical political and social transformation. Ending with Mao's death in 1976, the Revolution is remembered by historians of science both for its persecution of intellectuals and for its protagonists' articulation of a participatory, popular, distinctively socialist approach to science (Schmalzer 2006, 186–7). During this period, an effective schistosomiasis treatment campaign, helped by improved testing

Figure 8 'Work hard to undertake the Patriotic Hygiene Campaign!'. This 1963 poster in Chinese and Korean demonstrates the longevity of these campaigns. Foregrounded are a variety of health workers: street sweepers, latrine diggers, disinfectant sprayers, and fly swatters. Image courtesy of the National Library of Medicine, Bethesda, MD.

methods and drug delivery as well as expanded access to care, treated millions of patients (Gross 2016, 145–62, 167–74).

The Cultural Revolution was a moment of great prominence for rural medical workers. The barefoot doctor programme – perhaps the most famous aspect of public health associated with China –originated in a patchwork set of grassroots responses to the collapse of state rural health systems after the Great Leap Forward. In 1965, a nationwide effort to support these responses sent urban physicians to the countryside (Gross 2018, 339; Zhou 2020, 192–3, 202–12; see Figure 9). A new kind of medicine, synthesising Maoist ideals with Chinese and Western practices, emerged as a result. In contrast to the pre-1949 work of C. C. Chen (now teaching at the Sichuan Medical College in Chengdu) to place rural health in the hands of a small group of highly educated physicians, barefoot doctor programmes trained many medical workers in the basics of Chinese and Western medicine. Although the PRC government ostensibly defined barefoot doctors in terms of their dual roles as workers and healers, it also facilitated their professionalisation. The state created a coherent identity for barefoot doctors by minimising group conflicts and marginalising competition from alternative

Figure 9 'Go to the countryside to serve the 500 million peasants'. This 1965 poster depicts a barefoot doctor. Image courtesy of the National Library of Medicine, Bethesda, MD.

traditions like religious healing (Fang 2012, 160–1) – although select folk medical traditions persisted and were in some cases integrated into the work of the barefoot doctors (Zhou 2020, 119–21). Patients and local governments valued expertise despite the central state's efforts to de-emphasise it, giving rise to a symbiotic relationship in which barefoot doctors provided political protection and local knowledge to elite urban physicians; in exchange, the latter provided expertise and education to the former (Gross 2018). Western medicine eventually came to dominate rural areas, in no small part because it was easier for barefoot doctors to learn and use than the often voluminous and complex prescriptions of Chinese medicine. For instance, a 1969 reduction in pharmaceutical prices, as well as renewed state efforts to distribute basic medical instruments like stethoscopes and thermometers, popularised Western medicine among barefoot doctors in the villages outside Hangzhou. In contrast, barefoot doctors were reluctant to use Chinese drugs because they were difficult to cultivate, identify, and process (Fang 2012, 101–4).

Although new training programmes sought to expand access to medicine, other interests worked to limit the availability of information about disease and epidemics during the Maoist period, as the PRC exerted rigorous controls over communication of public health intelligence. In coastal Zhejiang, for example, responses to the El Tor cholera pandemic in the early 1960s referred to cholera as 'No. 2 disease' in correspondence to avoid panic and maintain order. The central government's management of this episode ultimately combined pre-existing systems to require vaccination certificates for travel with quarantine mandates to produce a lasting public health strategy for epidemic control, which emphasised strict information control alongside mass mobilisation (Fang 2021, 16–19).

Control of reproduction, as well as disease, also featured in health governance during the Maoist period. Initially, the PRC's adoption of Stalinism brought with it Marxist and Soviet pro-natalism: the belief that in socialist systems, populations were valued and valuable labour resources. Yet Mao's own statements on population could be contradictory and unclear; his changeable attitude on the subject created a climate of fear and a lack of any fixed agenda until after his death in 1978 (Greenhalgh 2008, 52–4). Some trends are observable, however, including key steps in the implementation of birth control, one of the most significant factors in the decrease of China's population growth rate over the twentieth century (Greenhalgh and Winckler 2005, 5–8, 315). Contraceptives became widely available in the 1960s, with intrauterine devices (IUDs) claiming the greatest popularity following a period of experimentation in hospitals and medical universities. By the end of that decade, research groups in China had developed some of the first low-dose oral contraceptive pills in the world, and these were being manufactured and promoted widely (Banister 1987, 171). After 1970, premier Zhou Enlai and development-minded allies implemented a 'later–longer–fewer policy' to lower the birth rate, limiting urban couples to two children and rural couples to three. It was in this campaign that many of the coercive methods now identified with the post-1978 one-child policy were forged: specifically, the deployment of birth planning workers in each village, urban work unit, and neighbourhood. These personnel kept track of women's reproductive status and could pressure those who did not conform to relevant quotas and norms to get abortions, sterilisations, or contraception (Whyte, Wang, and Cai 2015, 150).

Public health during the Maoist era constituted a key form of governance. It was enacted through mass campaigns that connected to broader political and social movements, whether the Patriotic Hygiene Campaign's responses to fears stemming from Chinese involvement in the Korean conflict, or the barefoot doctors' emergence as a response to the exigencies of the Great Leap Forward. In these connections between medicine and a broader body politic, we also see the enactment of new power dynamics. As the state's ability to conduct expansive health campaigns grew, so did the establishment of power over its citizens' health and biologies, not least by virtue of controlling information about the spread of epidemics or through the enforcement of limits on reproductive decision-making. This assertion of biopower connected to struggles for geopolitical power in the context of the Cold War.

3.4 Medical Diplomacy as Cold War Competition

The existence of the Republic of China on Taiwan provided a compelling reason for the PRC to involve itself in international health. Because the Nationalist Party claimed political authority over all of mainland China, from the 1950s Taiwanese participation in international organisations or exchanges directly challenged the legitimacy of the CCP. Both the ROC and PRC sought acknowledgement by other states as the sole legitimate government of 'one China' that included the mainland and Taiwan. And in the 1960s and 1970s, both governments identified medical aid as a powerful means to cultivate transnational political relationships.

After the end of the Second World War, as a new wave of Chinese migration from the mainland took root on Taiwan, American norms and practices of medicine converged with and replaced the Japanese colonial model. As had been the case with the flight to Chongqing in 1937, following the Nationalist Party to Taiwan were physicians, professors, and students, all of whom would help rebuild medical infrastructure after the war. For example, the National Defense Medical Center, a military medical training institute established by Robert Lim (林可勝, also Lin Kesheng or Lim Kho-seng), transferred to Taiwan in 1948. There it became a centre for medical education and served a student body including Overseas Chinese from South-East Asia with the support of the United States government (Soon 2020a, 181–7). The Republican state oversaw a provincial sanitary board, prefectural sanitary offices, and rural township health stations. The success of colonial vaccination regimes in accustoming the populace to routine interventions in their bodily health facilitated the imposition of this new medical administration (Chin 1998, 326–31). So did American aid: in the late 1940s and 1950s, education, standards of practice, and professional organisation were all remade in the American mould, in part through organisations like the Sino–American Joint Commission on Rural

Reconstruction, which helped establish rural health stations across the island (Chin 1998; Liu 2012, 161–2). Arguably, post-war medicine in Taiwan thus remained imperial in nature, as a protectorate of the United States in the new Cold War logic of containing Chinese communism (Liu 2012, 164–6).

The influence of the United States extended to Taiwan's involvement in international health. By the post-war era, American public health had decisively endorsed global strategies that prioritised focused and highly technologised interventions as a means of gaining allies in the struggle to contain the spread of communism (Porter 2006, 1668–9; Packard 2016, 113). Taiwan was not only a recipient of aid, but also actively participated in efforts to contain the PRC's influence in the developing world. Providing medical assistance to 'Third World' countries not yet under the influence of socialist states was one means of limiting mainland political influence on the global stage. Public health was also a key area of competition between the ROC and PRC for political legitimacy and recognition during the Cold War. After the Bandung Conference of 1955, which brought together newly independent Asian and African states with the shared vision of promoting socio-economic cooperation against imperialism or neo-colonialism, South-East Asia, Latin America, and especially Africa became important battlegrounds for recognition between the PRC on the mainland and the ROC on Taiwan.

Demonstrating engagement with health on an international level became important for both governments that claimed authority over 'one China'. The ROC focused its aid efforts on Africa, supported by American funds and aligned with WHO agendas. In 1959, the government on Taiwan announced an International Cooperation Program that provided agricultural aid, particularly to peasant farmers, alongside diplomatic cooperation with newly decolonised states, in an attempt to contain efforts on the Communist mainland to gain foreign allies. The Ministry of Foreign Affairs launched this programme, known as Operation Vanguard, in 1961 with the dispatch of a fifteen-person agricultural team to Liberia. The programme relied on American financial support, ultimately sending 922 experts to Africa and bringing over 400 Africans to Taiwan during the 1960s and 1970s (Hsieh 1985, 307–11; Altorfer-Ong 2014, 234–5). Its focus was agriculture, though it included veterinary and medical care programmes in Ethiopia, Liberia, and Libya, and remains operational today as the Taiwan International Cooperation Development Fund (Hsieh 1985, 307–11; Cheng 1994, 172; Alexander 2016, 556). The Taiwanese government also established aid programmes that included medical equipment, staff, and training exchanges in Latin America (Alexander 2014).

These initiatives faded as Taiwan's rulers encountered difficulties on the global political scene. In 1971, following rapprochement with the United

States under Richard Nixon, the PRC rejoined the UN as the sole representative of China, resulting in the expulsion of the ROC. As a UN affiliate, the WHO followed suit, welcoming the PRC in 1972 and ejecting the ROC (Siddiqi 1995, 110–12; Zhou 2017, 146). Its expulsion from the UN and WHO in the 1970s meant that Taiwan was excluded from the networks that had supported its health internationalism. And non-aligned nations had increasingly turned to a new benefactor, the PRC, for aid.

In the 1960s and 1970s, PRC medical diplomacy did not just compete for influence and acknowledgement with the ROC; it also promoted a distinctive socialist approach to rural health. In Africa, especially, PRC diplomats emphasised shared experiences of anti-colonial conflict and the desire to build bilateral relationships based on equality and friendship, rather than unequal intervention (Strauss 2009, 779–80). Medical aid most often manifested on the ground in teams of physicians, supplies, educational materials, and occasionally student-exchange programmes. For instance, in 1962 the PRC sent twenty-one tons of medical supplies along with wheat and steel to newly independent Algeria (Larkin 1971, 54, 94). This marked the beginning of a long programme of medical assistance, which included collaborations in acupuncture work and the pharmaceutical industry (Zou 2019). Two years later, PRC representatives signed a treaty agreeing to medical cooperation with North Vietnam, complementing its provision of military assistance in opposing the American-backed South Vietnamese government (Yan 2015, 128). In the same year, physicians helped establish a health programme in the United Republic of Tanzania that trained local medical personnel, built a medical laboratory, administered hospitals, and conducted village health demonstrations (Altorfer-Ong 2014, 244–71). From the early 1960s to the early 2000s, over 15,000 Chinese doctors and other medical personnel travelled to 47 African nations as part of cooperative programmes (Ogunsanwo 1974, 90; Youde 2010, 159). The collaborations continued despite the outbreak of the Cultural Revolution in 1966. All these efforts bore diplomatic fruit: by the end of the 1960s, fourteen African states established formal relations with the PRC, acknowledging it as the sole authority over one China (Foreign Ministry of the People's Republic of China 2004). Aside from bilateral aid, the PRC also mobilised Chinese medical tradition to conduct medical diplomacy at the level of high politics. Acupuncture practitioners treated numerous heads of socialist states, sometimes literally: Chinese acupuncture specialists conducted cataract removal operations on North Korean Supreme Leader Kim Il Sung and Cambodian Prime Minister Penn Nouth (Su 2021, 149–50). The success of these procedures gave therapeutic prestige to acupuncture in the socialist context.

3.5 More Than Barefoot Doctors: Chinese Contributions to Primary Health Care

Throughout the 1970s, the PRC actively promoted its system of rural medical care not only as an appropriate solution for the health challenges of the 'developing world', but also as a model for international health more broadly. The formal readmission of the PRC to the WHO in 1972 provided an opportunity for Chinese diplomats to present a model of medical administration that could offer an alternative to Euro–American practices of international health, which had been found wanting by many practitioners (Lee 1997). Building on broader critiques of Western biomedicine as irrelevant and perniciously elitist, international health experts accused their discipline of having inappropriately adopted top-down, one-size-fits-all, highly technological strategies to resolve complex social problems in public health, as in the case of WHO's recent failed efforts to eradicate malaria (Cueto 2004, 1864). As a result of these critiques of the status quo, as well as its own promotional efforts, the PRC became an increasingly popular model for international health in the Western world. At the same time, Chinese medicine – a term encompassing a diverse range of practices and theories – grew in popularity as a form of alternative therapy around the world.

After rapprochement between the PRC and the United States began in the 1970s, the two nations launched diplomatic exchanges in a range of fields. Scientific disciplines had long provided a major arena for multilateral interactions and played a major role in the 1978 re-establishment of formal Sino–American diplomatic relations (Barrett 2020; Millwood 2021). In 1972 an inaugural medical delegation from the PRC arrived in the United States on an 'unofficial mission' funded by the Rockefeller Foundation and partners (Su 2021, 152). Likewise, the Ministry of Health invited delegations from Europe and North America to visit the PRC; these groups typically consisted of researchers and physicians selected for their sympathetic views towards communism and China. The visitors were shown carefully curated scenes of the integration of Chinese and Western medical traditions via acupuncture anaesthesia, barefoot doctors, and other programmes, all of which were designed to demonstrate the successes of Chinese public health – and, by extension, the governmental successes of the PRC (Su 2018, 78). For instance, in 1972, the Cambridge biochemist Dorothy Needham kept a diary of a visit to Guangzhou in which she was shown two operations using 'acupuncture analgesia'. She wrote: 'Both patients perfectly calm; man smiled & waved to us when he got up. Baby cried & waved arms & legs as soon as breathing induced. Shown to mother, who smiled happily' (Needham 1972, 7–8). A 1975 documentary film produced under the auspices of the United States Agency for International Development captured

Figure 10 'The Barefoot Doctors of Rural China.' Courtesy of PublicResource.
Org. http://www.cambridge.org/Brazeltonfigure12

many of these successful episodes on camera, showing detailed footage of
barefoot doctors in village communes (Li 1975) (see Figure 10).

Visitors gave fulsome praise to the systems of rural medicine that the PRC
had shown them, suggesting China as a model for other nations and indeed
global health organisations to follow. Philip Lee, professor of social medicine at
the University of California–San Francisco, reported after a 1973 trip to the
PRC that 'the priority accorded public health programs and a clear set of
guiding principles' offered lessons for American health care (Lee 1974, 432).
Victor and Ruth Sidel, a physician and social worker, respectively, who travelled to the PRC in 1971 and 1972 (Zhou 2017, 140–1), sang the praises of the
barefoot doctors, concluding,

> A summary of China's achievements in transforming the delivery of medical
> care since 1949 shows an interweaving of three main threads: decentralization,
> demystification and continuity with the past. Following a pattern that many
> students of community medicine would be happy to see more widely emulated
> in Western countries, the delivery of medical care in China begins at the lowest
> possible level in both the city and the countryside. (Sidel and Sidel 1974, 23)

China seemed to offer an ideal archetype for 'primary health care', an increasingly popular concept which had probable roots in Christian missionary experiences in the 1960s and which combined local leadership, grassroots labour,
mass education, and preventive work (Cueto 2004, 1865).

The Chinese case ultimately articulated a model of primary health care that attracted worldwide consensus. A 2008 WHO publication asserted plainly that 'China's barefoot doctors were a major inspiration to the primary health care movement' (Cui 2008, 914). This movement culminated in the Alma-Ata Declaration of 1978, a resolution that set forth primary health care as the chief new direction for WHO. The Chinese delegate to the WHO, Wang Guizhen (王桂珍), had proposed a conference dedicated to this topic in 1976; the Soviet Union firmly supported the idea, but not in solidarity so much as competition with the PRC, offering significant financial backing to claim sponsorship of the conference. Therefore, the city of Alma-Ata (now Almaty), in the Kazakh Soviet Socialist Republic (now Kazakhstan) and a site of considerable Soviet medical intervention, was selected to host the historic meeting (Zhou 2017, 148–9).

While PRC representatives were promoting state medical systems within the discipline of international health, medicine from the Chinese-speaking world was moving around the world in very different networks and audiences. This, too, was partly due to the CCP's formulation of a new, systematised 'Traditional Chinese Medicine' (TCM), presenting Chinese medicine in a way that could be packaged and disseminated neatly (Hsu 1999, 6–8; Taylor 2005). One effect of this systematisation was the growing association of Chinese medicine with gradual, processual efficacy and, therefore, a focus on treatment of chronic illness – often as a means of complementing emergency medicine more frequently based on Western biomedical approaches (Karchmer 2015, 188–9, 209).

The use of Chinese medicine, especially to treat chronic illnesses that resisted biomedical intervention, had a long history in the West but rose to prominence in the 1960s and 1970s when disillusionment with the power of biomedicine led to growing interest in holistic, alternative therapeutic traditions (Barnes 2013, 284–320; Shelton 2019, 232–3). Acupuncture gained particular popularity in Europe and North America after the PRC publicised its use of acupuncture anaesthesia to visiting delegations in the early 1970s (Whorton 2002, 245–70; Hsu 2008, 479). The apparent success of this procedure made it a focus of considerable American interest, to the extent that debates over the legitimacy of acupuncture anaesthesia provided a means to discuss broader geopolitical conflicts (Baum 2021, 501–2). The PRC and its approach to TCM was not the only source of such knowledge; Taiwan, Hong Kong, and Overseas Chinese communities offered alternative sources of medical knowledge and authority, and in fact new waves of immigration from China since 1949 had provided medical staff to serve the rise in acupuncture's popularity (Barnes 2013, 286–9; Shelton 2019, 219, 251). Mei Zhan argues that Chinese medicine has been, and is still, constantly made and remade through such historicised, trans-local encounters (Zhan 2009). Physicians of Chinese medicine sought markets in spaces outside strict regulation in biomedical frameworks, and to these ends strategically exploited Orientalist tropes to gain patients while also seeking common ground with practitioners of allopathic Western biomedicine (Shelton 2019, 244–7). Contemporary practitioners of TCM continue to strategically use 'miracles' to build professional reputations and negotiate knowledge production; the marginalisation of this medical knowledge renders the efficacy of Chinese medicine miraculous, and allowed it to be 'worlded' as Chinese science in the 1960s and 1970s (Zhan 2009, 93, 103).

As a form of alternative medicine, Chinese practices of acupuncture and herbal drugs did not only appeal to New Agers. In the 1970s, members of the American Black Panther Party, which devoted considerable resources and attention to health care in Black communities as part of its struggle for social justice (Nelson 2011), adopted acupuncture as a means of pain management. For Black Panthers such as Torbert Small, part of the appeal of acupuncture lay in its relationship to Maoist politics of socialist revolution. In 1972, Small and other Party members travelled to the PRC to survey China's medical model in situ. Much like other delegations, the Black Panthers were shown acupuncture anaesthesia, barefoot doctors, and other means of integrating Chinese and Western medicine. Yet where other medical delegations were mostly inspired to initiate biomedical research collaborations in the form of professional conferences and laboratory experimentation, the Black Panthers enthusiastically instituted programmes to promulgate acupuncture theory and methods, and thereby empower African-American communities long disenfranchised from public health authority (Barnes 2013, 296–8; Meng 2021, 896–900).

As this and other episodes in this section suggest, far from a period of isolation and seclusion, the decades following the Second World War represented a historical moment of remarkable transnational exchange for Sinophone societies in the medical sphere. Most strikingly, the PRC under Mao found medicine fruitful ground for diplomatic engagement, promoting its own approach to medical epistemology and rural health management even as it received and offered medical aid in projects to improve bilateral relations with other socialist and post-colonial states. These engagements ultimately resonated with the disciplines of international and global health outside of which they had developed – demonstrated most clearly in the adoption of primary health care as a guiding policy for WHO. Yet these developments did not totally succeed in dislodging older understandings of China as a pathogenic environment.

In 1968, an avian influenza pandemic struck Hong Kong. The British colonial government's response to the outbreak – soon known as 'Hong Kong flu' – drew upon ongoing work in epidemiological surveillance and virology to articulate new ideas of pandemic preparedness as a continuous state of being requiring constant surveillance, and disease as an ecological concept bringing together environmental, biological, and social processes (Peckham 2020, 446). The outbreak also returned the attention of international health experts to the Chinese-speaking world as a site of dangerous zoonotic disease emergence. Even though subsequent decades would present a very different image of China to the world, as a model for rural health care and the source of Chinese medicine, the 1968 episode presaged a characterisation that would come to define the last decades of the twentieth century, recasting old visions of China as a source of disease in new vocabularies of epidemiology.

4 Post-Socialist Pandemics in Global China

The PRC's involvement in international and global health outlasted the revolutionary socialist period. This section considers the roles that the Sinophone world played in global health between the 1980s and 2010s, and the ramifications of this recent history for the present day. In the PRC, the economic, social, and political transformations of the 1980s and 1990s eroded the rural medical infrastructures that had become a model for global health at Alma-Ata. They also set the stage for new interactions between corporations, the state, and individuals that in turn changed the relationships connecting humans, animals, and diseases. The sequestration of Taiwan from WHO continued to contribute to its isolation from global health communities, while PRC epidemiologists found themselves excluded from such communities in more subtle ways. The 2003 eruption of a novel coronavirus, SARS-CoV-1, lay bare structural shortcomings in health systems across the Sinophone world. The episode energised a major reorganisation of epidemiology in the PRC, largely designed to avert the possibility of a similar scenario re-emerging – yet the pandemic outbreak of Covid-19 has suggested the difficulty of that task.

4.1 After Mao: Processes of Marketisation, Rapprochement, and Worlding

The end of the 1970s was a key turning point in the PRC's involvement in international health. In the span of just a few years, Mao Zedong's death in 1976 ended the Cultural Revolution. Chinese health systems were canonised as a model for primary health care through the Alma-Ata Declaration in 1978; and the rise to power of Deng Xiaoping (邓小平) in the same year marked the beginning of a new era of political and social transformation, often called 'economic reform and opening-up' (*gaige kaifang* 改革開放), that included greater integration with global economic and political networks. However, these transformations sometimes worked at odds with one another. Ironically, a collectivist, grassroots approach to public health in China became an international model just as the influence of Maoist collectivism on social, economic, and political systems there was coming to an end.

That tension found global resonance when international health experts redrew the dream of 'health for all' as an unattainable fantasy. In 1979, the Rockefeller Foundation held a conference at Bellagio, Italy, which promoted 'selective primary health care': an approach which claimed to make a start at implementing the methods endorsed at Alma-Ata, but in reality offered a thoroughly alternative approach. Selective primary health care turned its back on sweeping reforms with underspecified methods. Instead, it favoured limited interventions that largely continued traditional emphases on targeted technological approaches such as immunisation – an intervention that received widespread support following the 1980 near-total eradication of smallpox. In the early 1980s, UNICEF adopted the priorities set by selective primary health care, as did the World Bank, an increasingly important funder and supporter of international health (Cueto 2004, 1868–71).

Meanwhile, in the PRC, the rural health programmes which had gained global acclaim were being steadily dismantled in the wake of Deng Xiaoping's economic policies (Duckett 2011). In the early 1980s, a reimbursement policy allowed villagers to bypass poorly equipped and underfunded union clinics, resulting in a 'dumb-bell-shaped' medical hierarchy in which barefoot doctors (at the bottom) and county hospitals (at the top) became increasingly important. Although new licensing requirements and rural reforms imposed during the 1980s forced many barefoot doctors to quit practising medicine, those who remained developed stronger professional identities because licensing examinations had given them useful credentials (Fang 2012, 177–83). In urban areas, links between employment and health care provision were strained by growing variation and inequalities among employers and regions, as well as demographic changes brought about by migration to cities (Grogan 1995, 1074). In Shanghai, the growing commercialisation of health care fostered the establishment of 'expert clinics' marketing the services of famous doctors of Chinese medicine (Zhan 2009, 82). These trends generally worked to move medicine further into the private sector.

Despite these domestic challenges, the PRC continued to play an important role in international health, not least by virtue of its membership in WHO. This status came at the expense of Taiwan, which from 1997 pursued observer status at the World Health Assembly – the chief decision-making body in the WHO – although it only achieved this standing in 2009 for three years (Herington and Lee 2014, 2). The subsequent isolation of Taiwan meant that considerable achievements in health care there were excluded from global health discussions and policymaking. For instance, although the island's government successfully introduced a national health insurance scheme in 1995 that offered universal coverage and significant patient choice among Chinese and Western traditions, these experiences were overlooked by broader communities of global health (Chen 2020, 11–14).

The global connections of Chinese medicine also persisted through the final decades of the twentieth century. The worldwide spread of TCM and resultant entanglements of hybrid medical knowledge-making practices articulated a process Mei Zhan has called 'worlding', in which 'Chinese medicine' refers to a spectrum of practices made by highly localised trans-cultural interactions (Zhan 2009, 7; Furth 2011, 12–25; Barnes 2013, 338–9). As travel to mainland China became easier, Euro–American students displaced those from Asia, Africa, and Latin America in schools of Chinese medicine. These developments contributed to the ongoing involvement of the PRC state in projects of medical diplomacy, especially as Chinese investments in African economies expanded during the 1990s (Zhan 2009, 180; Hsu 2013).

Medicine in China went global in the 1980s in another, very different way: the exploitation of Chinese populations as research subjects by Western biomedical agents. For example, epidemiological research on cancer in the PRC had gained prominence during the 1970s and led to extensive collaboration between Chinese and American colleagues, providing transnational foundations for the growth and transformation of biotechnology in the PRC. This research, characteristically for the Cultural Revolution era, had featured mass mobilisation of peasants by barefoot doctors and local cadres to organise low-cost, non-invasive screenings and projects to reduce risk factors for cancer; between 1973 and 1975, a nationwide survey investigated cancer mortality across the country. Even though specialised cancer research clinics and laboratories had been operating since the late 1950s, it was this mass epidemiological movement that appealed to foreigners. During the 1980s, a series of conferences in the United States allowed Chinese researchers to share their findings about environmental exposures and nutritional deficiencies in populations across the PRC, visit laboratories, and learn new biomedical techniques. American researchers worked with Chinese partners to conduct studies on cancer incidence as it related to risk factors; in the process, Chinese people became increasingly and materially valuable to US scientists as 'biocapital', providing objects of study and analysis (Jiang

Global China

2018, 83–4, 88–92). In this respect, the PRC's population resembled those in other parts of the 'developing world', which became attractive sites for experimental clinical trials after the American Food and Drug Administration enacted increasingly strict oversight rules for domestic research in the 1960s and 1970s (Petryna 2009, 61–85).

4.2 Controlling Populations: Demographic and Epidemiological Transformations

The transition to a market economy brought with it socio-economic and demographic transformations. New forms of population control affected these trends. Although they were often coercive and implemented unevenly across the nation, the anti-natalist reproductive policies of the 1970s had been effective. They reduced population growth from nearly six births per woman (estimated over a lifetime) in 1970 to 2.7–2.8 in 1980. Given this outcome, the persistence of coercive methods in the 1980 implementation of the one-child policy made it a strategy 'based on politics and pseudoscience, rather than on necessity, much less on good demography' (Whyte, Wang, and Cai 2015, 152, 159 n. 3). The one-child policy was the brainchild of Soviet-trained missile scientist Song Jian (宋健). Song and other specialists in cybernetics, the science of control and communications in complex machine systems, developed a keen interest in China's population – despite not having any experience in demographic research – because Deng Xiaoping encouraged defence scientists to turn their attention to the nation's economic problems after Mao's death (Greenhalgh 2008, 125–68). Song engineered a policy that restricted births to one child per urban couple and two per rural couple (if the first was a daughter), with exceptions for minority peoples. (White 2006, 111–69). Eugenic ideals were incorporated into the one-child policy through projects such as the sterilisation of developmentally disabled individuals (Chung 2011, 15–24). Susan Greenhalgh and Edwin Winckler have claimed that these policies made China 'the world's most notable case of the rapid politicization of population, and a case in which regulation has encompassed not only the quantity of population but also its quality' (Greenhalgh and Winckler 2005, 29).

Control over populations and their biologies was not always so easy. As farming became less profitable and industry provided more jobs, marketisation stimulated mass migration from the countryside to the cities. However, the household registration (*hukou* 戶口) system, which still governs a variety of state entitlements, did not support such flexibility or circulation. Transferring one's registration to a city was a difficult and restricted enterprise. Consequently, many rural *hukou* holders who migrated to cities did so illegally. They became known as the 'floating population' (*liudong renkou* 流動人口): not tied to the cities by their household registration, no longer anchored to their rural home towns, and therefore existing at the margins of social systems. The floating population became a marginalised group ripe for association with disease transmission.

Sexually transmitted diseases were one epidemiological consequence of migration to cities, as women from rural areas pursued sex work that was in increasing demand from growing populations of urban labourers. In the early years of the PRC, prostitution had been outlawed and those who worked in the trade sent to reformatories, with a focus on controlling activity in Shanghai. The incidence of sexually transmitted diseases decreased significantly, to the point that the PRC declared the total elimination of venereal disease in 1964 (Dikötter 1993, 344–5; Ruan 2010). The 1980s saw a rapid reversal of these trends. By the late 1980s, HIV began to spread through the borderlands of south-west China and South-East Asia, following geographies of intravenous drug production and trade as well as sex work and migrant labour (Peckham 2016, 266–7). Over time, it spread across the Sinophone world.

In the United States, the HIV/AIDS crisis was a catalyst for change in which patient activists asserted agency in pursuing research and novel therapies. The epidemic played out differently in the PRC. Yunnan province, in the far south-west and bordering Vietnam, Myanmar, and Laos, was the official epicentre of the epidemic in China. State officials associated the disease with ethnic minorities that constituted an important part of the provincial population, stigmatising these minorities as sexually promiscuous in a nexus of racialised discrimination not uncommon in the history of medicine (Hyde 2007, 7). However, official narratives tended to elide a major means of transmission: contaminated blood, often through practices associated with selling blood plasma, a common trade in China in the 1990s.

Although selling blood had existed as a practice in earlier decades, the marketisation and deregulation of the 1980s and 1990s had a major impact on this trade. As small-scale farming became increasingly unsustainable thanks to rising taxes and material costs, many village officials, especially in Henan province, promoted and organised the selling of blood to commercial companies as a means for cash-strapped families to recoup some of their losses. Historian Robert Peckham notes that 'the selling of blood to service a nascent biotechnology industry hungry for human albumin became another dimension of a global market in which products manufactured in China depended on a "floating" rural population to provide cheap labor' (Peckham 2016, 275). Local organisers, or 'blood heads', profited from recruiting villagers to participate (Anagnost 2006, 518; Peckham 2016, 271). Because the needles and tubes used in collecting blood were often reused, and blood was re-infused to donors once it had been pooled and the valuable materials like albumin filtered out, the rate of blood-borne infections of donors skyrocketed (Anagnost 2006, 517). Those infections included hepatitis B, hepatitis C, and HIV.

Population control, sexually transmitted infections, and the transmission of disease through selling blood suggest that the transition to the post-Mao era gave rise to novel epidemiological patterns, exacerbated by efforts on the part of rural and impoverished populations to adapt to de-collectivisation policies. These trends had global ramifications. The harshness of the one-child policy contributed to feminist ambivalence about population control (Bashford 2018, 518–19). And China's experiences of HIV/AIDS displaced familiar narratives in which the disease became a problem primarily experienced by populations in Africa and Latin America, suggesting instead that the issues of stigmatisation and construction of foreign Others as disease carriers are widespread and not limited to Euro–American actors (Hyde 2007).

4.3 Epidemic Entanglements: One Health and Wildlife Farming

The emergence of new industrial and commercial relationships connecting humans, animals, and microbes was another consequence of de-collectivisation and the PRC's transition to a post-socialist economy after 1978. In 1981, the government formally recognised the re-emergence of a Household Responsibility System in which local officials allocated land and production quotas to individual households as a replacement for production teams (Lin 1988, S201). Newly private householders returned to older practices of small-scale cultivation in which one farm might host a few pigs, chickens, and a handful of crops. Their harvests were then sold at local wet markets: lately infamous as much-maligned sites of Covid-19 transmission, but in reality widespread and variable settings where fresh foodstuffs are bought and sold across Asia (Schneider 2018, 237).

The end of collectivisation did not necessarily entail a reversion to older methods of agriculture on a large scale, however. For instance, in the case of pork, the organisation and execution of food production have been globalised, 'while "traditional" methods and knowledges have been marginalized' (Schneider 2018, 236). Indeed, the general trend in China from the reform era to the present has seen the emergence of fewer, larger, more commercialised farms. This development has received institutional support; for instance, in the early 1990s China's Ministry of Agriculture imported pigs belonging to breeds valued by global supply chains for their speedy maturation. In the late 1990s, premier Jiang Zemin led an initiative to provide state subsidies, tax breaks, and other support to industrial agriculture firms labelled 'dragon head enterprises' (*longtou qiye* 龙头企业). These firms sourced and processed crops and meat from rural household cultivators. In addition to PRC state support, they also received foreign investments from private equity firms like Goldman Sachs (Schneider 2018, 235, 238).

Post-1978 rural and agricultural transformations intersected in unexpected ways with biosecurity programmes that emerged during the same period in international health. The decades following the successful eradication of small-pox saw a concern in global health with pre-emptively identifying and controlling infectious diseases as pandemic threats (Brown, Cueto, and Fee 2006: 69). International health experts also called attention to the importance of considering the health of animals in conjunction with that of humans, describing the need for 'One Health': collaborative work uniting veterinary and medical professions in cross-species epidemic control and research (Gibbs 2014, 87). As pandemic preparation was translated into the 'idiom of rural development', the UN Food and Agriculture Organization, as well as the Veterinary Bureau of the PRC, proposed that industrialisation of rural Chinese agriculture would also improve its biosecurity (Fearnley 2020, 67). Yet the economic pressures brought about by pandemic prevention could elicit paradoxical responses by farmers that increased the risk of pathogenesis and environmental damage. For instance, at Poyang Lake in Jiangxi province, duck farmers let their animals graze freely to cut feed costs, which raised the potential for interspecies transfer of novel influenza strains. The search by WHO teams and Chinese partners for the origins of influenza pandemics in China, starting in earnest in the 1980s, changed scientists' understanding of the disease itself, leading them towards an ecological view of influenza. Laboratory work on viral phylogenetics combined with broad claims about agricultural practices in south China, specifically the cultivation of free-grazing ducks, to produce claims that the PRC was a disease epicentre (Fearnley 2020).

The industrialisation of agriculture had ramifications for the involvement of animals in therapeutic medicine as well as disease transmission. Deng Xiaoping's rise to power not only signalled the state's turn towards 'reform and opening-up' in the realm of production and trade, but also towards a re-emphasis on expert-led science and technology. The Four Modernizations policy, proposed as early as 1963 but formally launched by Deng in 1978, sought to promote development in agriculture, industry, defence, and science. In service of the first, the state encouraged the growth of animal farming for drug production, blurring the lines between agriculture and medicine (Chee 2021, 143). One response to this call was the rapid expansion of bear farming in the 1980s. Although classical Chinese medical texts discussed bear bile (extracted from the gall bladder) as a therapeutic substance, and it was promoted as a Chinese traditional medicine, Japanese research had identified the active ingredient ursodeoxycholic acid and North Korean research had yielded the farming techniques that became prevalent in the PRC (Chee 2021, 142). Bear farming was thus the result of regional, transnational processes and studies, as well as domestic techniques.

By the middle of the 1980s, private businesses had established wildlife farms and nearly hunted to extinction over twenty species. There were several reasons for this explosion in popularity of the practice. Medicinal animals provided valuable fodder for export trade. Universities established experimental farms to study methods for domesticating wild animals and cultivating them for mass production in ways that would maximise yield. By 1983, the number of species identified as 'medicinal animals' had risen to 832; before 1949, the classical pharmaceutical text *Bencao gangmu* (本草綱目) had identified around 400 such animals (Chee 2021, 8). In 1988, the PRC passed the Wildlife Protection Law. This legislation set out a plan for protection of endangered species, management of nature reserves, and punishment of illegal hunting practices. It also set out the legal mechanisms to register and tax businesses dedicated to wildlife farming, and it presented the human use of animals as a rationale for their protection (Li 2007, 73–7, 82). The result was a law that attempted to regulate and limit the extraction of native and endangered species from China, but also codified and thus implicitly justified the mechanisms by which such extraction might reasonably take place. Wildlife farming therefore both contributed to the conservation of species and provided a means for human cultivators to profit and thrive. Wildlife farming is now a multi-million, if not billion, yuan industry (using PRC currency); as of 2013, the number of species classified as medicinal animals had almost tripled since 1983, standing at 2,341 (Li 2007, 89–90; Chee 2021, 8).

The growth of wildlife farming only amplified existing threats of disease flow between animal and human populations. In 1997, an outbreak of avian influenza struck poultry markets in Hong Kong. The virus responsible, H5N1, was a novel strain that had originated in Guangdong province a year earlier. Consequently, culling of poultry was carried out on a massive scale – 1.5 million birds were killed over three days (Peckham 2016, 279). Frédéric Keck argues that Hong Kong, Singapore, and Taiwan used discussions on avian influenza as a means of negotiating the risks posed by the PRC and its lack of transparency in disclosing emergent zoonotic threats (Keck 2020, 3). By the turn of the century, industrial poultry farming, especially in south China but across South-East Asia, had been identified as a zone of intensive farming where zoonotic transmission of disease from birds to humans posed a significant threat to public health. Although large firms that enrolled smallholders in such enterprises created the conditions of poor sanitation and crowding that are generally thought to give rise to zoonotic transmission, traditional small-scale farming methods have more frequently been blamed for such outbreaks by media outlets and multilateral organisations calling for the modernisation of these industries (Peckham 2016, 281). Now, in the wake of Covid-19, the stakes of this connection are high: it seeks to assign blame for the conditions that encouraged zoonotic transmissions of several novel coronaviruses to human populations, most notably SARS-CoV-1 in 2003 and SARS-CoV-2 in late 2019.

4.4 Anticipating, Researching, and Controlling Contemporary Epidemics

The first novel coronavirus to originate in China and reach epidemic proportions, SARS-CoV-1, emerged in November 2002. First identified as atypical pneumonia and suspected to be a novel strain of influenza, the initial outbreak occurred in Guangdong province. Then, an infected physician's stay in a Hong Kong hotel transmitted the disease to individuals who carried it abroad to Vietnam, Singapore, and Canada. Epidemiologists and virologists came to think that the disease probably originated in horseshoe bats, known to be a natural reservoir of coronaviruses. It was transmitted to humans via an intermediary species, possibly the masked palm civet cat, native to East and South-East Asia and eaten in China (Murray 2006, 17–19, 23; Hu et al. 2017). A specific set of multispecies entanglements is thus believed to have caused SARS, in which transgressive links between the habitats of wild animals and the bodies of middle-class consumers escaped the control of health administration and resulted in epidemic calamity (Zhan 2005).

In 2003, the PRC's response to SARS was consistent with precedents set in previous decades. It featured tight information control and stringent epidemic prevention measures imposed after the disease aroused the attention of broader publics. Like SARS-CoV-2, the virus that causes Covid-19, at the time of its outbreak no vaccines or drugs existed for SARS-CoV-1. So the strategies that were most effective in controlling the novel coronavirus, then as now, were historic ones – namely, quarantine and contact tracing (Peckham 2016, 287). The PRC state sought to control news about the crisis even as it amplified its information gathering, significantly under-reporting the number of patients affected by the disease (Jakes 2003), although residents of south China used text messaging on mobile phones and internet messaging boards to circumvent news blackouts and censorship. Once the cover-up was revealed to global news media, the PRC launched a health campaign that imposed strict quarantines, criminalised activities that might facilitate disease transmission, and employed military metaphors in propaganda promoting public health interventions (Peckham 2016, 288–92).

Looking beyond the actions of the central state reveals a telling range of responses to SARS in 2003. The epidemic provided an opportunity for TCM practitioners to seek to demonstrate the effectiveness of their methods. For instance, doctors of Chinese medicine in Guangdong province played a major role in the treatment of SARS patients there. Defining SARS-CoV-1 as a hot-wind disorder within the etiological category of *wenbing* (溫病, warm diseases), they used herbal medicines alongside biomedical therapies like respirators and corticosteroids (Hanson 2010, 233, 238). In the process they claimed the value of Chinese medicine for treating acute as well as chronic illnesses (Hanson 2010, 243; Karchmer 2015, 210–11).

Another important response emerged in the epidemiological profession. SARS triggered the re-envisioning of Chinese public health as a professional, biomedical, and highly technological discipline. The outbreak of SARS in 2003 had coincided with ongoing reformation of public health in the PRC, and epidemiologists took advantage of the new urgency and prominence attributed to disease control to acquire funding and support for their profession, asserting their chief goal to be the prevention of a similar outbreak in the future. To these ends, 'epidemic prevention stations' were transformed into 'centres for disease control' modelled on the American Centers for Disease Control and Prevention (CDC), which took a very aggressive approach to contact tracing, quarantine, and other public health measures. Yet when swine flu was transmitted to the PRC in 2009, the implementation of these measures was criticised by foreign observers at WHO as overly harsh, suggesting the continued exclusion of Chinese epidemiologists from full and equitable membership in the global health community (Mason 2016, 7–24).

The SARS outbreak also altered the field of global health more broadly. It led the WHO to take unprecedented steps to assert transnational power in its effort to control this new infectious disease, issuing daily online updates and travel warnings advising individuals against travel to regions affected by the illness (Tseng and Wu 2010, 261). And in 2003, even as global health professionals stressed the need for collaboration across borders, polities affected by the outbreak defined their borders in new, biomedically significant ways. For example, Taiwan issued a home quarantine order for travellers arriving from SARS-stricken places; this order was as much a response to political and social dissatisfaction as to epidemic conditions (Tseng and Wu 2010, 257–8, 267). Because the ROC had been expelled from the WHO, its attempts to notify the Organization of SARS cases in Taiwan were delayed and direct technical assistance was impeded (Herington and Lee 2014, 7). The political and social pressure to protect populations' health created by SARS incentivised WHO and state actors to adopt an extremely conservative approach to disease control that falsely assumed total safety from epidemic risk was possible (Tseng and Wu 2010, 270–1).

Both the PRC and Taiwan have mounted projects involving global institutions to fight recent epidemics – none more strikingly than Covid-19. In December 2019, medical staff in Wuhan began to report a novel respiratory infection, soon to become known as SARS-CoV-2. The early weeks and months of the virus' circulation, as well as the first quarantines and lockdowns, coincided with what has been described as the largest internal migration in the world: the annual journeys made by many migrant workers from the cities where they work to their rural home towns for the Lunar New Year (Choy and Xie 2020). The Wuhan municipal government was slow to respond to this emerging viral threat. In some cases, most infamously that of physician Li Wenliang (李文亮), efforts to raise awareness about the spread of this novel coronavirus were actively suppressed (Kynge, Yu, and Hancock 2020). The breakdown of primary care systems resulted in overcrowded hospitals in Wuhan and other cities. A BBC programme describes the experiences of Chinese-American director Hao Wu and colleagues in Wuhan who produced a film about the 2020 lockdowns in that city (BBC 2021).

These factors combined disastrously with the ability of the virus to infect many via asymptomatic carriers to facilitate the rapid spread of Covid-19, the disease associated with the virus, in the first months of 2020. Domestic discontent over the handling of the pandemic quickly arose within a population upon whom the CCP had long impressed its responsibility to protect the people's health (Zhang 2020).

The international ramifications of the outbreak were immediately apparent. As the pandemic spiralled into a global crisis in March 2020, foreign observers were quick to find fault with the Chinese government for failing to confine the disease within its borders (Hamid 2020). By contrast, the ROC on Taiwan took early steps to control Covid-19 that proved remarkably successful, drawing on 2003 experiences with SARS to establish a unified Central Epidemics Command Center, implementing rapid quarantine and personal protective equipment (PPE) policies, and strategically engaging with PRC physicians and officials (Soon 2020b). More generally, the identification of SARS-CoV-2 with China and Chinese people fanned the flames of xenophobia and racism around the world, so much so that US President Donald Trump called it the 'Wuhan virus'. As this Element goes to press, in 2022, most nations of the world have ended quarantine and vaccine requirements related to Covid-19, signalling attempts to ideate an end to the pandemic – yet harmful stereotypes targeting people of East Asian backgrounds have persisted.

4.5 Conclusion: 'Lessons from History'?

Hopefully, readers who have made it this far will see that there are many readily apparent connections between past and present in Chinese responses to Covid-19. The stigmatising association of people of Asian descent with the origins and spread of Covid-19, for instance, has many precedents. The history of medicine has documented many case studies of minority and migrant populations being blamed for spreading disease (Kraut 1995; Leavitt 1996; Shah 2001). Indeed, one *Wall Street Journal* article went so far as to invoke the hoary 'sick man of Asia' trope mentioned in Section 1 (Mead 2020). In terms of health policy, mass mobilisation campaigns implementing hygienic reform, efforts to control information about epidemics, and projects of medical diplomacy – all of which rose to prominence as health strategies during the 1950s and 1960s – constituted important dimensions of the PRC's response to Covid-19. After initial obfuscations, largely blamed on local administrations, a centrally organised and well-publicised mobilisation of manpower manifested in January 2020. Its outcomes included the recruitment of neighbourhood committee leaders and volunteers to monitor quarantines and the transport of construction workers to Wuhan to rapidly erect new hospitals. The military language used to describe this mobilisation, as well as its great scale, echo the Patriotic Hygiene Campaigns discussed in the previous section.

Other aspects of the response were not necessarily so loudly trumpeted. The imperative to carefully control information about infectious diseases – both to gather as much epidemiological knowledge as possible, and to control access to that data – was apparent in early 2020. Local Wuhan and Hubei authorities suppressed the circulation of information about Covid-19 in the outbreak's early months. Most notably, authorities blocked the efforts of the physician Li Wenliang to raise awareness of the virus' spread (Kynge, Yu, and Hancock 2020). This is an approach that we have seen before, in the PRC's efforts to control information about the El Tor cholera outbreak in the 1960s, as well as efforts to conceal the scale of the SARS epidemic in 2003. Finally, in March 2020, widely circulated photographs of Chinese medical teams disembarking from airplanes and unloading crates containing hygienic supplies to donate to Italy were evocative of promotional materials for the medical teams that the PRC sent to decolonised nations as part of its programmes of medical diplomacy in the 1960s (Zou 2021). In 2021, as immunisation programmes got underway across the globe, 'vaccine diplomacy' saw the PRC sending shipments of vaccines made by state-owned enterprise Sinopharm to Hungary, Iran, and other nations with which its diplomats sought to improve bilateral relationships (Lee 2021).

Historical precedents for current strategies are not just limited to recent decades. The vaccines made by Sinopharm, for instance, were developed at an organisation – the Beijing Tiantan Institute of Biological Products, now a subsidiary of China National Biotec Group – which identifies as the direct successor of the National Epidemic Prevention Bureau, established in 1919 (discussed in Section 1.3). The Bureau's manufacture of vaccines to serve policies of mass immunisation has thus persisted from the Second Sino–Japanese War to the present. Many have attributed the swift adoption of face masks in Taiwan and the PRC to the precedent set by Wu Liande's innovations in the Manchurian pneumonic plague of 1910–11. The development of TCM protocols to treat Covid-19 reflects the professionalisation of Chinese medicine and its integration into Chinese health care more broadly (Zhao et al. 2021). And ambivalent participation by the PRC in international health meetings and discussions focusing on Covid-19 reflects the long history of Chinese efforts to engage with international health organisations, even as those organisations have identified China as a source of disease. Likewise, the historically contingent bifurcation of the PRC and Taiwan has continued to shape global health decision-making. Taiwan won praise from observers for its swift response to Covid-19: in the absence of WHO guidance, it dispatched physicians to Wuhan to learn more about the disease, undertook mass surgical mask production in January 2020 to supply the population, and acted swiftly to ban visitors from Hubei and then China by early February 2020. The 2003 experience of SARS – specifically the WHO's refusal to provide support and problems supplying PPE – had been critical to this rapid response insofar as the ruling Democratic People's Party (DPP) decided early on not to rely on WHO aid and to mobilise supply chains for face masks. Also important were agreements facilitating medical exchanges worked out between the PRC and Taiwan in previous years, when the latter was led by Nationalist Party members, as well as Taiwanese living in Wuhan who provided early warnings (Soon 2020b, 648–52).

I have just listed a series of historical precedents: trends and events that bear some similarity and even direct connections to each other, despite a separation of decades and sometimes centuries. What conclusions might be drawn from the existence of these parallels? We must remain attuned to the complexities of such comparisons. Throughout the Covid-19 pandemic, historians of medicine have called attention to the need to avoid facile 'lessons from history' (Lynteris 2020; Lachenal and Thomas 2020). It is easy for participants in global health to deploy historical precedents to amplify their self-presentations of good governance, either by claiming to correct past wrongs or to replicate former successes. Wayne Soon points out, for example, that 'though Chinese media explicitly invoked Wu [Liande] in early 2020 as an inspiration for its exemplary pandemic control, the Chinese government shared little of Wu's conviction that the successful control of the pandemic required international trust, awareness, and cooperation' (Soon 2020a, 198). So history offers the potential to identify crucial differences in context, intention, and impact that demonstrate the affordances and contingencies of specific policies, as well as explanations for their adoption and evolution.

Most of the trends described in this Element have suggested the enduring and extensive exchanges of Chinese peoples, economies, and intellectual communities with the rest of the world. The medical pluralism long characteristic of Chinese healing practices, for instance, survived existential challenges and found new markets in a twentieth-century world that increasingly sought alternatives to biomedical paradigms. And the epizootic epidemics of the twenty-first century are best described as incited by the advent of industrial agriculture, backed by multinational corporate interests and serving globalising economic networks whose links appear to grow ever more interdependent. Yet trends over the twentieth century have also upheld the significance of the national over the regional and the global. Chinese governments have tended to increase power over citizens' lives – biopower – as expressed through large-scale campaigns featuring intensive hygienic interventions. In the wake of Covid-19, a key site of such intervention has proved to be national borders. The 1930 establishment of a National Quarantine Service with Wu Liande at its head once offered a powerful statement that the young Republic of China had taken control of its borders and clawed back 'an integral part of its health infrastructure' from foreign imperial powers (Yip 1995, 117). Today, borders again hold great significance in the face of global travel controls – and both the PRC and Taiwan restricted entry for foreign visitors in their efforts to forestall community transmission of Covid-19. Although xenophobic stereotypes have long identified China as a pathogenic place whose peoples' movements might spread disease, to Chinese populations it is now the rest of the world which represents a pandemic threat.

References

Ahn, B. (2013). Reinventing Scientific Medicine for the Socialist Republic: The Soviet Psycho-Prophylactic Method of Delivery in 1950s China. *Twentieth-Century China* **38**(2): 139–55.

Akami, T. (2016). A Quest to Be Global: The League of Nations Health Organization and Inter-Colonial Regional Governing Agendas of the Far Eastern Association of Tropical Medicine, 1910–25. *The International History Review* **38**(1): 1–23.

Alexander, C. (2014). *China and Taiwan in Central America*. New York: Palgrave Macmillan.

Alexander, C. (2016). Taiwan's Public Diplomacy. In G. Schubert, ed., *Routledge Handbook of Contemporary Taiwan*. London: Routledge, pp. 544–58.

Altorfer-Ong, A. (2014). Old Comrades and New Brothers: A Historical Re-examination of the Sino–Zanzibari and Sino–Tanzanian Bilateral Relationships in the 1960s. PhD dissertation, London School of Economics and Political Science.

Amelung, I. (2020). Introduction. In I. Amelung, ed., *Discourses of Weakness in Modern China: Historical Diagnoses of the 'Sick Man of East Asia'*. Frankfurt: Campus Verlag, pp. 9–22.

Anagnost, A. S. (2006). Strange Circulations: The Blood Economy in Rural China. *Economy and Society* **35**(4): 509–29.

Anderson, M. R., Smith, L., and Sidel, V. W. (2005). What Is Social Medicine? *Monthly Review* **56**(8): 27–34.

Anderson, W. and Pols, H. (2012). Scientific Patriotism: Medical Science and National Self-Fashioning in Southeast Asia. *Comparative Studies in Society and History* **54**(1): 93–113.

Andrews, B. J. (2013). The Republic of China. In T. J. Hinrichs and L. L. Barnes, eds., *Chinese Medicine and Healing: An Illustrated History*. Cambridge, MA: Harvard University Press, pp. 209–38.

Andrews, B. J. (2014). *The Making of Modern Chinese Medicine, 1850–1960*. Vancouver: UBC Press.

A Rural Health Experiment in China. (1930). *Milbank Memorial Fund Quarterly Bulletin* **8**(4): 97–108.

Asen, D. (2009). 'Manchu Anatomy': Anatomical Knowledge and the Jesuits in Seventeenth- and Eighteenth-Century China. *Social History of Medicine* **22**(1): 23–44.

Balińska, M. A. (1991). Ludwik Rajchman, International Health Leader. *World Health Forum* **12**: 456–65.

Banister, J. (1987). *China's Changing Population*. Stanford, CA: Stanford University Press.

Barnes, L. L. (2013). A World of Chinese Medicine and Healing: Parts One and Two. In T. J. Hinrichs and L. L. Barnes, eds., *Chinese Medicine and Healing: An Illustrated History*. Cambridge, MA: Harvard University Press, pp. 284–378.

Barnes, N. E. (2018). *Intimate Communities: Wartime Healthcare and the Birth of Modern China, 1937–1945*. Oakland: University of California Press.

Barrett, G. (2020). Minding the Gap: Zhou Peiyuan, Dorothy Hodgkin, and the Durability of Sino–Pugwash Networks. In A. Kraft and C. Sachse, eds., *Science, (Anti-)Communism and Diplomacy: The Pugwash Conferences on Science and World Affairs in the Early Cold War*. Leiden: Brill, pp. 190–217.

Basch, P. F. (1999). *Textbook of International Health*. Second ed. Oxford: Oxford University Press.

Bashford, A. (2004). *Imperial Hygiene: A Critical History of Colonialism, Nationalism and Public Health*. Basingstoke, UK: Palgrave Macmillan.

Bashford, A. (2018). World Population from Eugenics to Climate Change. In N. Hopwood, R. Flemming, and L. Kassell, eds., *Reproduction: Antiquity to the Present Day*. Cambridge: Cambridge University Press, pp. 505–19.

Baum, E. (2021). Acupuncture Anesthesia on American Bodies: Communism, Race, and the Cold War in the Making of 'Legitimate' Medical Science. *Bulletin of the History of Medicine* **95**(4): 497–527.

BBC. (2021). *Inside the Hospitals of Lockdown Wuhan*. Podcast. www .bbc.co.uk/programmes/p095y1z4.

Borowy, I. (2009a). *Coming to Terms with World Health: The League of Nations Health Organisation 1921–1946*. Frankfurt: Peter Lang.

Borowy, I. (2009b). Thinking Big – League of Nations Efforts towards a Reformed National Health System in China. In Borowy, I., ed., *Uneasy Encounters: The Politics of Medicine and Health in China, 1900–1937*. Frankfurt: Peter Lang, pp. 205–28.

Brazelton, M. A. (2019). *Mass Vaccination: Citizens' Bodies and State Power in Modern China*. Ithaca, NY: Cornell University Press.

Bretelle-Establet, F. (1999). Resistance and Receptivity: French Colonial Medicine in Southwest China, 1898–1930. *Modern China* **25**(2): 171–203.

Brown, T. M. and Fee, E. (2008). The Bandoeng Conference of 1937: A Milestone in Health and Development. *American Journal of Public Health* **98**(1): 42–3.

Brown, T. M., Cueto, M., and Fee, E. (2006). The World Health Organization and the Transition from 'International' to 'Global' Public Health. *American Journal of Public Health* **96**(1): 62–72.

Bu, L. (2009). Public Health and Modernisation: The First Campaigns in China, 1915–1916. *Social History of Medicine* **22**(2): 305–19.

Bu, L. (2017). *Public Health and the Modernization of China, 1865–2015.* London: Routledge.

Bullock, M. B. (1980). *An American Transplant: The Rockefeller Foundation and Peking Union Medical College.* Berkeley: University of California Press.

Campbell, T. and Sitze, A. (2013). Introduction. In T. Campbell and A. Sitze, eds., *Biopolitics: A Reader.* Durham, NC: Duke University Press, pp. 1–40.

Carrai, M. A. (2019). *Sovereignty in China: A Genealogy of a Concept Since 1840.* Cambridge: Cambridge University Press.

Chai, O. and Ch'ae, U. (2017). Interstate Relations in East Asia and Medical Exchanges in the Late Eleventh Century and Early Twelfth Century. *Korean Studies* **41**: 30–51.

Chee, L. P. Y. (2021). *Mao's Bestiary: Medicinal Animals and Modern China.* Durham, NC: Duke University Press.

Chen [Ch'en], C. C. (1936). The Rural Public Health Experiment in Ting Hsien, China. *Milbank Memorial Fund Quarterly* **14**(1): 66–80.

Chen, C. C. (1989). *Medicine in Rural China: A Personal Account.* Berkeley: University of California Press.

Chen, L. (陈兰彬) (2018). *Chen Lanbin ji: wu: shifu, yinglian* (陈兰彬集:伍:诗赋,楹联) [The Collected Works of Chen Lanbin: Five: Poems and Couplets]. Guangzhou: Guangdong renmin chubanshe.

Chen, Y. F. (2020). Taiwan and the World Health Assembly/World Health Organization: Perspectives from Health Services and Research. *International Journal of Taiwan Studies* **3**: 10–27.

Cheng, T. Y. (1994). Foreign Aid in ROC Diplomacy. In B. Lin and J. Myers, eds., *Contemporary China and the Changing International Community.* Columbia: University of South Carolina Press, pp. 170–86.

Chin, H. (1998). Colonial Medical Police and Postcolonial Medical Surveillance Systems in Taiwan, 1895–1950s. *Osiris* **13**: 326–38.

Choa, G. H. (1990). *'Heal the Sick' Was Their Motto: The Protestant Medical Missionaries in China.* Hong Kong: The Chinese University Press.

Choy, G. and Xie, E. (2020). As China Goes Back to Work after Lunar New Year, Will the Coronavirus Spread Even More Rapidly? *South China Morning Post*, 4 February. https://bit.ly/3V2PfOj.

Chung, Y. J. (2010). Eugenics in China and Hong Kong: Nationalism and Colonialism, 1890s–1940s. In A. Bashford and P. Levine, eds., *The Oxford*

Handbook of the History of Eugenics. Oxford: Oxford University Press, pp. 258–73.

Chung, Y. J. (2011). The Postwar Return of Eugenics and the Dialectics of Scientific Practice in China. *Middle Ground Journal* **3**: 1–50.

Chung, Y. J. (2014). Better Science and Better Race? Social Darwinism and Chinese Eugenics. *Isis* **105**(4): 793–802.

Cueto, M. (2004). The Origins of Primary Health Care and Selective Primary Health Care. *American Journal of Public Health* **94**(11): 1864–74.

Cueto, M. (2020). The History of International Health: Medicine, Politics, and Two Socio-Medical Perspectives, 1851 to 2000. In C. McInnes, K. Lee, and J. Youde, eds., *The Oxford Handbook of Global Health Politics*. Oxford: Oxford University Press, pp. 19–36.

Cueto, M., Brown, T.M., and Fee, E. (2019). *The World Health Organization: A History*. Cambridge: Cambridge University Press.

Cui, W. (2008). China's Village Doctors Take Great Strides. *Bulletin of the World Health Organization* **86**(12): 914–15.

David, M. (2018). Female Gynecologists and Their Birth Control Clinics: Eugenics in Practice in 1920s–1930s China. *Canadian Bulletin of Medical History* **35**(1): 32–62.

Dikötter, F. (1993). Sexually Transmitted Diseases in Modern China: A Historical Survey. *Genitourin Med* **69**: 341–5.

Dr. H.S. Gear: Newly Appointed Secretary-General, World Medical Association. (1961). *South African Medical Journal* **35**(23): 465.

Duckett, J. (2011). *The Chinese State's Retreat from Health: Policy and the Politics of Retrenchment*. Abingdon, UK: Routledge.

Echenberg, M. (2007). *Plague Ports: The Global Urban Impact of Bubonic Plague, 1894–1901*. New York: New York University Press.

Elman, B. A. (2008). Sinophiles and Sinophobes in Tokugawa Japan: Politics, Classicism, and Medicine during the Eighteenth Century. *East Asian Science, Technology and Society: An International Journal* **2**(1): 93–121.

Evans, S. (2020). Coronavirus Has Finally Made Us Recognise the Illegal Wildlife Trade Is a Public Health Issue. *The Conversation*, 17 March. https://bit.ly/3EE4XcE.

Fang, X. (2012). *Barefoot Doctors and Western Medicine in China*. Rochester, NY: University of Rochester Press.

Fang X. (2021). *China and the Cholera Pandemic: Restructuring Society under Mao*. Pittsburgh, PA: University of Pittsburgh Press.

Farquhar, J. and Lai, L. (2021). *Gathering Medicines: Nation and Knowledge in China's Mountain South*. Chicago, IL: University of Chicago Press.

Fearnley, L. (2020). *Virulent Zones: Animal Disease and Global Health at China's Pandemic Epicenter.* Durham, NC: Duke University Press.

Foreign Ministry of the People's Republic of China. (2004). Diplomatic Ties between China and African Countries, viewed 18 October 2021. www .fmprc.gov.cn/ce/ceza/eng/zghfz/zfgx/t165322.htm.

Fu, J.-C. (2016). Houses of Experiment: Making Space for Science in Republican China. *East Asian Science, Technology and Society: An International Journal* **10**(3): 269–90.

Furth, C. (2011). The AMS/Paterson Lecture: Becoming Alternative? Modern Transformations of Chinese Medicine in China and in the United States. *Canadian Bulletin of Medical History* **28**(1): 5–41.

Gamsa M. (2006). The Epidemic of Pneumonic Plague in Manchuria, 1910–1911. *Past & Present* **190**: 147–83.

Gao X. (2014). Foreign Models of Medicine in Twentieth-Century China, trans. S. Wilms, X. Gao, and B. Andrews. In B. Andrews and M. B. Bullock, eds., *Medical Transitions in Twentieth-Century China.* Bloomington: Indiana University Press, pp. 173–211.

Gear, H. S. (1937). A Plea for Improved South African Medical and Vital Statistics. *South African Medical Journal* **11**(5): 149–54.

Ghosh, A. (2020). *Making It Count: Statistics and Statecraft in the Early People's Republic of China.* Princeton, NJ: Princeton University Press.

Gibbs, E. P. J. (2014). The Evolution of One Health: A Decade of Progress and Challenges for the Future. *Veterinary Record* **174**(4): 85–91.

Golvers, N. (2011). The Jesuits in China and the Circulation of Western Books in the Sciences (17th–18th Centuries): The Medical and Pharmaceutical Sections in the SJ Libraries of Peking. *East Asian Science, Technology, and Medicine* **34**: 15–62, 64–85.

Grant, J. B. (1935). Principles for the China Program. Rockefeller Archive Center, Rockefeller Foundation records, projects, RG 1.1, series 601, box 14, folder 143.

Greenhalgh, S. (2008). *Just One Child: Science and Policy in Deng's China.* Berkeley: University of California Press.

Greenhalgh, S. and Winckler, E. A. (2005). *Governing China's Population: From Leninist to Neoliberal Biopolitics.* Stanford, CA: Stanford University Press.

Grogan, C. M. (1995). Urban Economic Reform and Access to Health Care Coverage in the People's Republic of China. *Social Science & Medicine* **41**(8): 1073–84.

Gross, M. (2016). *Farewell to the God of Plague: Chairman Mao's Campaign to Deworm China.* Oakland: University of California Press.

Gross, M. (2018). Between Party, People, and Profession: The Many Faces of the 'Doctor' during the Cultural Revolution. *Medical History* **62**(3): 333–59.

Guénel, A. (2012). The 1937 Bandung Conference on Rural Hygiene: Toward a New Vision of Healthcare? In L. Monnais and H. J. Cook, eds., *Global Movements, Local Concerns: Medicine and Health in Southeast Asia*. Singapore: NUS Press, pp. 62–80.

Guo, Z. (郭作贵), ed. (1993). *Jinan nianjian 1993* (济南年鉴 1993) [Jinan Yearbook 1993]. Jinan: Jinan chubanshe.

Hamid, S. (2020). China Is Avoiding Blame by Trolling the World. *The Atlantic*, 19 March. https://bit.ly/3g5RkJ2.

Hanson, M. E. (2010). Conceptual Blind Spots, Media Blindfolds: The Case of SARS and Traditional Chinese Medicine. In A. K. C. Leung and C. Furth, eds., *Health and Hygiene in Chinese East Asia: Policies and Publics in the Long Twentieth Century*. Durham, NC: Duke University Press, pp. 228–54.

Harris, S. H. (1994). *Factories of Death: Japanese Biological Warfare 1932–45 and the American Cover-Up*. London: Routledge.

Harrison, M. (2016). Afterword. In A. Bashford, ed., *Quarantine: Local and Global Histories*. London: Palgrave, pp. 251–7.

Haynes, D. M. (2001). *Imperial Medicine: Patrick Manson and the Conquest of Tropical Disease*. Philadelphia: University of Pennsylvania Press.

Herington, J. and Lee, K. (2014). The Limits of Global Health Diplomacy: Taiwan's Observer Status at The World Health Assembly. *Globalization and Health* **10**(71): 1–9.

Hinrichs, T. J. (2013). The Song and Jin Periods. In T. J. Hinrichs and L. L. Barnes, eds., *Chinese Medicine and Healing: An Illustrated History*. Cambridge, MA: Harvard University Press, pp. 97–127.

Hsieh C.-C. (1985). *Strategy for Survival: The Foreign Policy and External Relations of the Republic of China on Taiwan, 1949–1979*. London: Sherwood.

Hsu, E. (1999). *The Transmission of Chinese Medicine*. Cambridge: Cambridge University Press.

Hsu, E. (2008). The History of Chinese Medicine in the People's Republic of China and Its Globalization. *East Asian Science, Technology and Society: An International Journal* **2**(4): 465–84.

Hsu, E. (2013). Chinese Medicine in Africa. In In T. J. Hinrichs and L. L. Barnes, eds., *Chinese Medicine and Healing: An Illustrated History*. Cambridge, MA: Harvard University Press, pp. 335–8.

Hu, B., Zeng, L.-P., Yang, X.-L., et al. (2017). Discovery of a Rich Gene Pool of Bat SARS-Related Coronaviruses Provides New Insights into the Origin of SARS Coronavirus. *PLoS Pathogens* **13**(11): e1006698.

Hyde, S. T. (2007). *Eating Spring Rice: The Cultural Politics of AIDS in Southwest China*. Berkeley: University of California Press.

Iijima, W. (2003). Spanish Influenza in China, 1918–20: A Preliminary Probe. In H. Phillips and D. Killingray, eds., *The Spanish Influenza Pandemic of 1918–19: New perspectives*. London: Routledge, pp. 101–9.

International Sanitary Conference. (1881). *Proceedings of the International Sanitary Conference Provided for by Joint Resolution of the Senate and House of Representatives*. Washington, DC: Government Printing Office.

International Sanitary Conference. (1885). *Protocoles et procès-verbaux de la Conférence sanitaire internationale de Rome, inaugurée le 20 mai 1885*. Rome: Impr. du Ministère des affaires étrangères.

International Sanitary Conference. (1897). *Conférence sanitaire internationale de Venise, 16 février–19 mars 1897: procès-verbaux*. Rome: Forzani et cie, imprimeurs du Sénat.

Jakes, S. (2003). Beijing's SARS Attack. *Time*, 8 April.

Jiang, L. (2018). Global Epidemiology, Local Message: Sino–American Collaboration on Cancer Research, 1969–1990. In P. Manning and M. Savelli, eds., *Global Transformations in the Life Sciences, 1945–1980*. Pittsburgh, PA: University of Pittsburgh Press, pp. 78–98.

Jiang, T. (江濤聲) (1934a). Sulian gonggong weisheng de shizhi (蘇聯公共衛生的實質) [The Essence of Soviet Public Health]. *Zhonghua yixue zazhi* **20**(11): 1393–1414.

Jiang, T. (江濤聲) (1934b). Sulian gonggong weisheng de shizhi (蘇聯公共衛生的實質(續完)[The Essence of Soviet Public Health (part 2)]. *Zhonghua yixue zazhi* **20**(12): 1489–1522.

Johnson, T. P. (2011). *Childbirth in Republican China: Delivering Modernity*. Lanham, MD: Rowman & Littlefield.

Karchmer, E. I. (2015). Slow Medicine: How Chinese Medicine Became Efficacious Only for Chronic Conditions. In H. Chiang, ed., *Historical Epistemology and the Making of Modern Chinese Medicine*. Manchester: Manchester University Press, pp. 188–216.

Keck, F. (2020). *Avian Reservoirs: Virus Hunters and Birdwatchers in Chinese Sentinel Posts*. Durham, NC: Duke University Press.

Knab, C. (2011). Plague Times: Scientific Internationalism and the Manchurian Plague of 1910/1911. *Itinerario* **35**(3): 87–105.

Kondō, S. (近藤昭二) and Wang, X. (王选), eds. (2019). *Riben shengwu wuqi zuozhan diaocha ziliao (quan 6 ce)* (日本生物武器作战调查资料(全6册) [Japanese Biological Weapons in Warfare: A Survey of Materials (6 vols.)]. Beijing: Shehui kexue wenxian chubanshe.

Kraut, A. M. (1995). *Silent Travelers: Germs, Genes, and the 'Immigrant Menace'*. Baltimore, MD: Johns Hopkins University Press.

Kuhn, P. A. (2008). *The Chinese among Others: Emigration in Modern Times*. Lanham, MD: Rowman & Littlefield.

Kynge, J., Yu, S., and Hancock, T. (2020). Coronavirus: The Cost of China's Public Health Cover-Up. *Financial Times*, 6 February. www.ft.com/content/fa83463a-4737-11ea-aeb3-955839e06441.

Lachenal, G. and Thomas, G. (2020). COVID-19: When History Has No Lessons. *History Workshop*, 30 March. www.historyworkshop.org.uk/covid-19-when-history-has-no-lessons/.

Larkin, B. (1971). *China and Africa, 1949–1970: The Foreign Policy of the People's Republic of China*. Berkeley: University of California Press.

Lazich, M. C. (2006). Seeking Souls through the Eyes of the Blind: The Birth of the Medical Missionary Society in Nineteenth-Century China. In D. Hardiman, ed., *Healing Bodies, Saving Souls: Medical Missions in Asia and Africa*. Amsterdam: Rodopi, pp. 59–86.

Leavitt, J. W. (1996). *Typhoid Mary: Captive to the Public's Health*. Boston, MA: Beacon Press.

Lee, P. R. (1974). Medicine and Public Health in the People's Republic of China. *Western Journal of Medicine* 120(5): 430–7.

Lee, S. (1997). WHO and the Developing World: The Contest for Ideology. In A. Cunningham and B. Andrews, eds., *Western Medicine as Contested Knowledge*. Manchester: Manchester University Press, pp. 24–45.

Lee, S. T. (2021). Vaccine Diplomacy: Nation Branding and China's COVID-19 Soft Power Play. *Place Branding and Public Diplomacy*. https://doi.org/10.1057/S41254-021-00224-4.

Lei, S. H. (1999). From *Changshan* to a New Anti-Malarial Drug: Re-networking Chinese Drugs and Excluding Chinese Doctors. *Social Studies of Science* 29(3): 323–58.

Lei, S. H. (2010). Sovereignty and the Microscope: Constituting Notifiable Infectious Disease and Containing the Manchurian Plague (1910–1911). In C. Furth and A. Leung, eds., *Health and Hygiene in Chinese East Asia*. Durham, NC: Duke University Press, pp. 73–106.

Lei, S. H. (2014). *Neither Donkey nor Horse: Medicine in the Struggle over China's Modernity*. Chicago, IL: University of Chicago Press.

Li, D. (1975). *The Barefoot Doctors of Rural China*. Online video clip. www.youtube.com/watch?v=1YvwVFC-TJY.

Li, P. J. (2007). Enforcing Wildlife Protection in China: The Legislative and Political Solutions. *China Information* 31(1): 71–107.

Lin, J. Y. (1988). The Household Responsibility System in China's Cultural Reform: A Theoretical and Empirical Study. *Economic Development and Cultural Change* **36**(S3): S199–S224.

Litsios, S. (2005). Selskar Gunn and China: The Rockefeller Foundation's 'Other' Approach to Public Health. *Bulletin of the History of Medicine* **79**(2): 295–318.

Litsios, S. (2011). John Black Grant: A 20th-Century Public Health Giant. *Perspectives in Biology and Medicine* **54**(4): 532–49.

Litsios, S. (2014). Revisiting Bandoeng. *Social Medicine* **8**(3): 113–28.

Liu, C.-L. (2017). Relocating Pastorian Medicine: Accommodation and Acclimatization of Pastorian Practices against Smallpox at the Pasteur Institute of Chengdu, China, 1908–1927. *Science in Context* **30**(1): 33–59.

Liu, S. (2009). *Prescribing Colonization: The Role of Medical Practices and Policies in Japan-Ruled Taiwan, 1895–1945*. Ann Arbor, MI: Association for Asian Studies.

Liu, S. (2012). From Japanese Colonial Medicine to American-standard medicine in Taiwan: A Case Study of The Transition in the Medical Profession and Practices in East Asia. In L. Bu, D. Stapleton, and K. Yip, eds., *Science, Public Health and the State in Modern Asia*. Abingdon, UK: Routledge, pp. 161–76.

Lo, M.-C. (2002). *Doctors within Borders: Profession, Ethnicity, and Modernity in Colonial Taiwan*. Berkeley: University of California Press.

Luesink, D. (2017). Anatomy and the Reconfiguration of Life and Death in Republican China. *Journal of Asian Studies* **76**(4): 1009–34.

Luesink, D. and Asen, D. (2019). Globalizing Biomedicine through Sino–Japanese Networks: The Case of National Medical College, Beijing, 1912–1937. In D. Luesink, W. H. Schneider, and D. Zhang, eds., *China and the Globalization of Biomedicine*. Rochester, NY: Boydell & Brewer, pp. 81–108.

Lüthi, L. M. (2008). *The Sino–Soviet Split: Cold War in the Communist World*. Princeton, NJ: Princeton University Press.

Lynteris, C. (2014). Epidemics as Events and as Crises: Comparing Two Plague Outbreaks in Manchuria (1910–11 and 1920–21). *Cambridge Journal of Anthropology* **32**(1): 62–76.

Lynteris, C. (2019). Tarbagan's Winter Lair: Framing Drivers of Plague Persistence in Inner Asia. In C. Lynteris, ed., *Framing Animals as Epidemic Villains: Histories of Non-Human Disease Vectors*. Cham: Palgrave Macmillan, pp. 65–90.

Lynteris, C. (2020). Didactic Historicism and the Historical Consciousness of Epidemics. *Somatosphere: Science, Medicine, and Anthropology*. https://bit.ly/3S4WAdg.

Manderson, L. (2009). Wireless Wars in the Eastern Arena: Epidemiological Surveillance, Disease Prevention and the Work of the Eastern Bureau of the

League of Nations Health Organisation, 1925–1942. In P. Weindling, ed., *International Health Organisations and Movements, 1918–1939*. Cambridge: Cambridge University Press, pp. 109–33.

Manela, E. (2010). A Pox on Your Narrative: Writing Disease Control into Cold War History. *Diplomatic History* **34**(2): 299–323.

Marks, S. (2014). Reflections on the 1944 National Health Services Commission: A Response to Bill Freund and Anne Digby on the Gluckman Commission. *South African Historical Journal* **66**(1): 169–87.

Mason, K. A. (2016). *Infectious Change: Reinventing Chinese Public Health after an Epidemic*. Stanford, CA: Stanford University Press.

Mead, W. R. (2020). China Is the Real Sick Man of Asia. *Wall Street Journal*, 3 February. www.wsj.com/articles/china-is-the-real-sick-man-of-asia-11580 773677.

Meng, E. (2021). Use of Acupuncture by 1970s Revolutionaries of Color: The South Bronx 'Toolkit Care' Concept. *American Journal of Public Health* **111**(5): 896–906.

Merkel-Hess, K. (2016). *The Rural Modern: Reconstructing the Self and State in Republican China*. Chicago, IL: University of Chicago Press.

Millwood, P. (2021). An 'Exceedingly Delicate Undertaking': Sino–American Science Diplomacy, 1966–78. *Journal of Contemporary History* **56**(1): 166–90.

Minden, K. (1994). *Bamboo Stone: The Evolution of a Chinese Medical Elite*. Toronto: University of Toronto Press.

Ministère des Affaires Étrangères. (1912). *Conférence Sanitaire Internationale de Paris, 7 Novembre 1911–17 Janvier 1912: Procès-Verbaux*. Paris: Imprimerie Nationale.

Mougey, T. (2017). Needham at the Crossroads: History, Politics and International Science in Wartime China (1942–1946). *British Journal for the History of Science* **50**(1): 83–109.

Murray, M. (2006). The Epidemiology of SARS. In A. Kleinman and J. L. Watson, eds., *SARS in China: Prelude to Pandemic?* Stanford, CA: Stanford University Press, pp. 17–30.

Nappi, C. (2009). Bolatu's Pharmacy: Theriac in Early Modern China. *Early Science and Medicine* **14**(6): 737–64.

Needham, D. (1972). China 1972. File GCPP Needham 5/1/13/1, Personal Papers of Dorothy Needham, Girton College Archive, Cambridge.

Nelson, A. (2011). *Body and Soul: The Black Panther Party and the Fight against Medical Discrimination*. Minneapolis: University of Minnesota Press.

Ogunsanwo, A. (1974). *China's Policy in Africa, 1958–71*. Cambridge: Cambridge University Press.

Packard, R. M. (2016). *A History of Global Health: Interventions into the Lives of Other Peoples*. Baltimore, MD: Johns Hopkins University Press.

Palmer, S. (2010). *Launching Global Health: The Caribbean Odyssey of the Rockefeller Foundation*. Ann Arbor: University of Michigan Press.

Pearson, J. L. (2018). *The Colonial Politics of Global Health: France and the United Nations in Postwar Africa*. Cambridge, MA: Harvard University Press.

Peckham, R. (2016). *Epidemics in Modern Asia*. Cambridge: Cambridge University Press.

Peckham, R. (2020). Viral Surveillance and the 1968 Hong Kong Flu Pandemic. *Journal of Global History* **15**(3): 444–58.

Petrie, G. F. (1912). An Epidemiological Review of the Epidemic of Pneumonic Plague in Northern China, 1910 to 1911. In R. P. Strong, ed., *Report of the International Plague Conference Held at Mukden, April, 1911*. Manila: Bureau of Printing, pp. 409–27.

Petryna, A. (2009). *When Experiments Travel: Clinical Trials and the Global Search for Human Subjects*. Princeton, NJ: Princeton University Press.

Pols, H. (2018). *Nurturing Indonesia: Medicine and Decolonisation in the Dutch East Indies*. Cambridge: Cambridge University Press.

Porter, D. (1999). *Health, Civilization and the State: A History of Public Health from Ancient to Modern Times*. London: Routledge.

Porter, D. (2006). How Did Social Medicine Evolve, and Where Is It Heading? *PLoS Medicine* **3**(10): 1667–72.

Porter, D. and Porter, R. (1988). What was Social Medicine? An Historiographical Essay. *Journal of Historical Sociology* **1**(1): 90–106.

Puente-Ballesteros, B. (2011). Jesuit Medicine in the Kangxi Court (1662–1722): Imperial Networks and Patronage. *East Asian Science, Technology, and Medicine* **34**: 86–162.

Rajchman, L. (1934). *League of Nations Council Committee on Technical Co-operation between the League of Nations and China: Report of the Technical Agent of the Council on his Mission in China, from the Date of his Appointment until April 1st, 1934*. Document C.157.M.66.1934, League of Nations, Geneva.

Rockefeller Foundation. (1934). Attached Note from Norma S. Thompson. Rockefeller Archive Center, Rockefeller Foundation records, projects, RG 1.1, series 601, box 14, folder 143.

Rockefeller Foundation. (1938). Minutes of the Rockefeller Foundation regarding the China program. Rockefeller Archive Center, Rockefeller Foundation records, projects, RG 1.1, series 601, box 14, folder 143.

Rogaski, R. (2004). *Hygienic Modernity: Meanings of Health and Disease in Treaty-Port China*. Berkeley: University of California Press.

Rogaski, R. (2021). The Manchurian Plague and COVID-19: China, the United States, and the 'Sick Man', Then and Now. *American Journal of Public Health* **111**(3): 423–9.

Ruan, Q. (2010). Reexamining the Abolitionist Movement against Prostitution in Shanghai after 1949. *Frontiers of History in China* **5**(3): 471–90.

Schmalzer, S. (2002). Breeding a Better China: Pigs, Practices, and Place in a Chinese County, 1929–1937. *Geographical Review* **92**(1): 1–22.

Schmalzer, S. (2006). Labor Created Humanity: Cultural Revolution Science on Its Own Terms. In J. W. Esherick, P. G. Pickowicz, and A. G. Walder, eds., *The Chinese Cultural Revolution as History*. Stanford, CA: Stanford University Press, pp. 185–210.

Schneider, M. (2018). Reforming the Humble Pig: Pigs, Pork and Contemporary China. In R. Sterckx, M. Siebert, and D. Schäfer, eds., *Animals through Chinese History: Earliest Times to 1911*. Cambridge: Cambridge University Press, pp. 233–43.

Shah, N. (2001). *Contagious Divides: Epidemics and Race in San Francisco's Chinatown*. Berkeley: University of California Press.

Shelton, T. V. (2019). *Herbs and Roots: A History of Chinese Doctors in the American Medical Marketplace*. New Haven, CT: Yale University Press.

Shen, C. (沈佳姍) (2015). Riben zai Manzhou jianli de mianyi jishu yanjiu jigou ji qi fangyi, 1906–1945 (日本在滿洲建立的免疫技術研究機構及其防疫, 1906–1945) [Immunology Institutes and Immunological Prevention Strategy in Manchuria during the Japanese Ruling Period, 1906–1945]. *Guoshiguan guan kan* **45**: 103–52.

Siddiqi, J. (1995). *World Health and World Politics: The World Health Organization and the UN System*. London: Hurst and Company.

Sidel, V. W. and Sidel, R. (1974). The Delivery of Medical Care in China. *Scientific American* **230**(4): 19–27.

Smith, L. (1999). Quakers in Uniform: The Friends Ambulance Unit. In P. Brock and T. P. Socknat, eds., *Challenge to Mars: Essays on Pacifism from 1918 to 1945*. Toronto: University of Toronto Press, pp. 243–55.

So, B. (苏基朗) (2012). You fa wu tian? Yan Fu yi 'tian yan lun' dui 20 shiji chu Zhongguo falü de yingxiang (有法无天?严复译《天演论》对 20 世纪初中国法律的影响) [An Immoral Law? Yan Fu's Translation of Evolutionary Theory and Its Influence on Chinese law in the Twentieth Century]. *Qinghua faxue* **6**(5): 128–42.

Solomon, S. G. (2017). Thinking Internationally, Acting Locally: Soviet Public Health as Cultural Diplomacy in the 1920s. In S. Grant, ed., *Russian and Soviet Health Care from an International Perspective: Comparing*

Professions, Practice and Gender, 1880–1960. Cham: Palgrave Macmillan, pp. 193–216.

Soon, W. (2014). Science, Medicine, and Confucianism in the Making of China and Southeast Asia – Lim Boon Keng and the Overseas Chinese, 1897–1937. *Twentieth-Century China* **39**(1): 24–43.

Soon, W. (2016). Blood, Soy Milk, and Vitality: The Wartime Origins of Blood Banking in China, 1943–45. *Bulletin of the History of Medicine* **90**(3): 424–54.

Soon, W. (2020a). *Global Medicine in China: A Diasporic History*. Stanford, CA: Stanford University Press.

Soon, W. (2020b). From SARS to COVID-19: Rethinking Global Health Lessons from Taiwan. *East Asian Science, Technology and Society: An International Journal* **14**(4): 647–55.

Strauss, J. (2009). The Past in the Present: Historical and Rhetorical Lineages in China's Relations with Africa. *China Quarterly* **199**: 777–95.

Strong, R. P. (1912). Report of the International Plague Conference Held at Mukden, April 1911. Manila: Bureau of Printing.

Su, J. (苏静静) (2018). Zhongguo yu shijie weisheng zuzhi hezuo zhong de shenfen zhuanbian: 1949–1978 (中国与世界卫生组织合作中的身份转变: 1949–1978) [The Commencement of Multilateral Health Diplomacy of People's Republic of China, 1949–1978]. *Zhongguo keji shi zazhi* **39**(1): 73–87.

Su, J. (苏静静) (2021). Diplomatie de la médecine traditionnelle chinoise en République Populaire de Chine: un atout dans la Guerre froide [Diplomacy of Traditional Chinese Medicine in the People's Republic of China: A Calling Card during Cold War], J. Ciaudo, trans. *monde(s)* **20**: 141–61.

Summers, W. C. (2012). *The Great Manchurian Plague of 1910–11: The Geopolitics of an Epidemic Disease*. New Haven, CT: Yale University Press.

Sze, S. (1982). *The Origins of the World Health Organization: A Personal Memoir, 1945–48*. Boca Raton, FL: L.I.S.Z. Publications.

Taylor, K. (2005). *Chinese Medicine in Early Communist China, 1945–63: A Medicine of Revolution*. London: RoutledgeCurzon.

The Sick Man of the Far East. (1905). *New York Times*, August 16.

Thompson, C. M. (2015). *Vietnamese Traditional Medicine: A Social History*. Singapore: NUS Press.

Tseng, Y. and Wu, C.-L. (2010). Governing Germs from outside and within Borders: Controlling 2003 SARS Risk in Taiwan. In A. K. C. Leung and C. Furth, eds., *Health and Hygiene in Chinese East Asia: Policies and Publics in the Long Twentieth Century*. Durham, NC: Duke University Press, pp. 255–72.

Van Vleet, S. A. (2015). Medicine, Monasteries and Empire: Tibetan Buddhism and the Politics of Learning in Qing China. PhD dissertation, Columbia University.

Velmet, A. (2020). *Pasteur's Empire: Bacteriology and Politics in France, Its Colonies, and the World*. Oxford: Oxford University Press.

Waitzkin, H., Iriart, C., Estrada, A., and Lamadrid, S. (2001). Social Medicine Then and Now: Lessons From Latin America. *American Journal of Public Health* **91**(10): 1592–1601.

Watt, J. R. (2014). *Saving Lives in Wartime China: How Medical Reformers Built Modern Healthcare Systems amid War and Epidemics, 1928–1945*. Leiden: Brill.

White, T. (2006). *China's Longest Campaign: Birth Planning in the People's Republic, 1949–2005*. Ithaca, NY: Cornell University Press.

Whorton, J. C. (2002). *Nature Cures: The History of Alternative Medicine in America*. Oxford: Oxford University Press.

Whyte, M. K., Wang, F., and Cai, Y. (2015). Challenging Myths about China's One-Child Policy. *China Journal* **74**: 144–59.

Wu, L. (1911). *Views of Harbin (Fuchiatien) Taken during the Plague Epidemic, December 1910–March 1911*. Shanghai: Commercial Press.

Wu, L. (1922). The Second Pneumonic Plague Epidemic in Manchuria, 1920–21. In L. Wu, ed., *North Manchurian Plague Prevention Service Reports (1918–1922)*. Tianjin: Tientsin Press, pp. 1–54.

Wu, L. ed. (1934). *Manchurian Plague Prevention Service Memorial Volume: 1912–1932*. Shanghai: National Quarantine Service.

Wu, L. (1959). *Plague Fighter: The Autobiography of a Modern Chinese Physician*. Cambridge: W. Heffer & Sons.

Wu, L., and Chun, J.W.H. (1922). The Recent Cholera Epidemic in China, 1919. In L. Wu, ed., *North Manchurian Plague Prevention Service Reports (1918–1922)*. Tianjin: Tientsin Press, pp. 181–96.

Yan, X. (阎学通) (2015). *Zhongguo yu zhoubian zhongdeng guojia guanxi* (中国与周边中等国家关系) [The Relations between China and Its Bordering States]. Beijing: Shehui kexue wenxian chubanshe.

Yip, K. C. (1995). *Health and National Reconstruction in Nationalist China: The Development of Modern Health Services, 1928–1937*. Ann Arbor, MI: Association for Asian Studies.

Youde, J. (2010). China's Health Diplomacy in Africa. *China: An International Journal* **8**(1): 151–63.

Zanasi, M. (2007). Exporting Development: The League of Nations and Republican China. *Comparative Studies in Society and History* **49**(1): 143–69.

Zhan, M. (2005). Civet Cats, Fried Grasshoppers, and David Beckham's Pajamas: Unruly Bodies after SARS. *American Anthropologist* **107**(1): 31–42.

Zhan, M. (2009). *Other-Worldly: Making Chinese Medicine through Transnational Frames*. Durham, NC: Duke University Press.

Zhang, T. (2020). How Much Could a New Virus Damage Beijing's Legitimacy? *ChinaFile*, 29 January. https://bit.ly/3T2DYvU.

Zhao, Z., Li, Y., and Zhou L., et al. (2021). Prevention and Treatment of COVID-19 Using Traditional Chinese Medicine: A Review. *Phytomedicine* **85**(153308): 1–7.

Zhou, T. (2019). *Migration in the Time of Revolution: China, Indonesia, and the Cold War*. Ithaca, NY: Cornell University Press.

Zhou X. (2017). From China's 'Barefoot Doctor' to Alma Ata: The Primary Health Care Movement in the Long 1970s. In P. Roberts and O.A. Westad, eds., *China, Hong Kong, and the Long 1970s: Global Perspectives*. Cham: Palgrave Macmillan, pp.135–57.

Zhou X. (2020). *The People's Health: Health Intervention and Delivery in Mao's China, 1949–1983*. Montreal: McGill-Queen's University Press.

Zhu, J. (朱建平) and Cao, L. (曹丽娟). (2009). Qing mo zhengfu yingdui jibing de xin jucuo (清末政府应对疾病的新举措) [New Measures by the Late Qing Government to Respond to Epidemics]. In Yu X. (余新忠), ed., *Qing yi lai de jibing, yiliao he weisheng: yi shehui wenhua shi wei shijiao de tansuo* (清以来的疾病，医疗和卫生:以社会文化史为视角的探索) [Disease, Medical Practice, and Public Health Since the Qing: An Exploration from the Perspective of Sociocultural History]. Beijing: Sanlian shudian, pp. 126–38.

Zou, D. (2019). Socialist Medicine and Maoist Humanitarianism: Chinese Medical Missions to Algeria, 1963–1984. PhD dissertation, Columbia University.

Zou, D. (2021). PRC Medical Internationalism: From Cold War to Covid-19. National University of Singapore Ariscope blog, 21 January. https://nus.edu/3z3rso7.

Acknowledgements

I would like to thank the manuscript's reviewers and the Global China series editor, Ching Kwan Lee, as well as Micah Muscolino, Simon Szreter, and Vinayak Chaturvedi, who edited some of the pieces in which I worked out early ideas. Joshua Nall's comments improved the manuscript tremendously. I am indebted to Chan Po-lin, Amy Cawthorne, Dora Vargha, Mary Fissell, Monica Green, Guido Alfani, Adam Tooze, John Manton, and Frank Snowden for productive conversations in the World Health Organization's Pandemic History Think Tank. Exchanges with Bogdan Iacob, Sarah Marks, and others involved with the Connecting3Worlds Project were very helpful. Special thanks go to Anin Luo, Eana Meng, Timothy Sim, and Yu Jia; Laura Stark's class on global health at Vanderbilt; Ke Ren's class on Chinese history at Holy Cross; seminars on history of medicine led by Dora Vargha at Exeter University and Jesse Olszynko-Gryn at Strathclyde University; participants in the MIT seminar 'History of Now – Plague and Pandemics'; and students associated with the Science Gallery – Bengaluru. All errors and translations are my own.

Cambridge Elements ☰

Global China

Ching Kwan Lee
University of California–Los Angeles

Ching Kwan Lee is professor of sociology at the University of California–Los Angeles. Her scholarly interests include political sociology, popular protests, labor, development, political economy, comparative ethnography, China, Hong Kong, East Asia and the Global South. She is the author of three multiple award-winning monographs on contemporary China: *Gender and the South China Miracle: Two Worlds of Factory Women* (1998), *Against the Law: Labor Protests in China's Rustbelt and Sunbelt* (2007), and *The Specter of Global China: Politics, Labor and Foreign Investment in Africa* (2017). Her co-edited volumes include *Take Back Our Future: An Eventful Sociology of Hong Kong's Umbrella Movement* (2019) and *The Social Question in the 21st Century: A Global View* (2019).

About the Series

The Cambridge Elements series Global China showcases thematic, region- or country-specific studies on China's multifaceted global engagements and impacts. Each title, written by a leading scholar of the subject matter at hand, combines a succinct, comprehensive and up-to-date overview of the debates in the scholarly literature with original analysis and a clear argument. Featuring cutting edge scholarship on arguably one of the most important and controversial developments in the 21st century, the Global China Elements series will advance a new direction of China scholarship that expands China Studies beyond China's territorial boundaries.

Cambridge Elements ☰

Global China

Elements in the series

Printed in the United States
by Baker & Taylor Publisher Services